THE BLACK CHRIST

The Bishop Henry McNeal Turner Studies in North American Black Religion

1. *For My People* by James H. Cone

2. *Black and African Theologies* by Josiah U. Young

3. *Troubling Biblical Waters* by Cain Hope Felder

4. *Black Theology USA and South Africa* by Dwight N. Hopkins

5. *Empower the People* by Theodore Walker, Jr.

6. *A Common Journey* by George C. L. Cummings

7. *Dark Symbols, Obscure Signs* by Riggins R. Earl, Jr.

8. *A Troubling in My Soul* by Emilie Townes

Editor:
  James H. Cone,
  Union Theological Seminary, New York

The purpose of this series is to encourage the development of biblical, historical, theological, and pastoral works that analyze the role of the churches and other religious movements in the liberation struggles of blacks in the United States and the Third World. What is the relationship between black religion and black peoples' fight for justice in the U. S.? What is the relationship between the black struggle for justice in the U. S. and the liberation struggles of the poor in Asia, Africa, Latin America, and the Caribbean? A critical investigation of these and related questions will define the focus of this series.

This series is named after Bishop Henry McNeal Turner (1834–1915), whose life and work symbolize the black struggle for liberation in the U. S. and the Third World. Bishop Turner was a churchman, a political figure, a missionary, a pan-Africanist — a champion of black freedom and the cultural creativity of black peoples under God.

The Bishop Henry McNeal Turner Studies
in North American Black Religion
Volume IX

THE BLACK CHRIST

Kelly Brown Douglas

ORBIS BOOKS

Maryknoll, New York 10545

Fifth Printing, February 1998

The Catholic Foreign Mission Society of America (Maryknoll) recruits and trains people for overseas missionary service. Through Orbis Books, Maryknoll aims to foster the international dialogue that is essential to mission. The books published, however, reflect the opinions of their authors and are not meant to represent the official position of the society.

Library of Congress Cataloging-in-Publication Data

Douglas, Kelly Brown.
   The black Christ / Kelly Brown Douglas.
      p.   cm. — (The Bishop Henry McNeal Turner studies in North American Black religion : vol. 9)
   Includes bibliographical references and index.
   ISBN 0-88344-939-0
   1. Jesus Christ—Afro-American interpretations.   2. Jesus Christ—Person and offices—History of doctrines.   3. Black theology—History.   4. Liberation theology—History.   5. Feminist theology—United States.   6. Afro-American women—Religious life.   I. Title.
II. Series.
BT304.912D68   1993
232'.089'96073—dc   93-35821
                                                                                    CIP

In Memory of my Grandmothers
Helen Vivian Dorsey
and
Virgie Brown
Two faithful churchwomen
in whose faces I could see Christ

CONTENTS

Acknowledgments   ix

Introduction   1
    Who Is the Black Christ?   6
    Is the Black Christ Enough?   7

Chapter 1
The Roots of the Black Christ   9
    Slaveholding Christianity and the White Christ   10
    Slave Christianity and the Black Christ   20
    Black Nationalists and the Color of Christ   30
    Early Black Literature and the Black Christ   32

Chapter 2
The Black Struggle and the Black Christ   35
    Martin Luther King, Jr., and the Black Christ   37
    Malcolm X and the Color of Christ   45

Chapter 3
The Theological Development of the Black Christ   53
    The Relationship between Blackness and Christ   55
    The Significance of Liberation and Reconciliation   64
    Violence or Nonviolence?   72

Chapter 4
A Critical Assessment of the Black Christ   78
    An Assessment of Each Claim   79
    Is the Black Christ Adequate?   84
    The Emergence of Womanist Theology   92

Chapter 5
A Womanist Approach to the Black Christ   **97**
   Laying a Womanist Foundation   97
   Something *More* about the Blackness of Christ   106
   The Womanist Black Christ Challenges Womanists and
      the Church   113
   The Black Christ from a Womanist Eye   116

Notes   **118**

Index   **132**

ACKNOWLEDGMENTS

This book is the result of the support and encouragement which I have received from many persons. Although the list is too long to mention them all, there are some who have been instrumental in this project coming to completion.

I must first thank David O. Woodyard, my mentor during my undergraduate studies at Denison University, for introducing me to Black theology.

I am also deeply grateful to Lawrence N. Jones, former Dean of Howard University School of Divinity, for giving me the time and scholarly support to work on this project in its early stages. I am most appreciative for his timely words of wisdom and expressions of love.

I have been blessed with a group of friends who have stood by me during this long journey with support and encouragement. I am particularly grateful to Joyce Rene Carter, Janie Dargan and Christine Wiley.

Lloyd J. Miller, my cousin and dear friend, has stuck by me from beginning to end and has done all those little things that make a difference.

I am eternally grateful to Dennis W. Wiley who painstakingly read through several drafts of this text always giving helpful advice.

Robert Ellsberg (Orbis Books) also provided critical editorial assistance and support.

I could never adequately express my gratitude to James H. Cone who has been my mentor, advisor and friend. He saw potential in me that I did not know I had. He has pushed me to get in touch with what it means to be Black and woman. He has supported me in innumerable ways with this project.

Above all, I thank my family without whom I could have done

nothing. I could never have come this far without the sacrifices of my parents William and Mary Brown. They created a home environment which has allowed each of their children to respond to God's call.

I am most thankful for the support, encouragement, and patience of my husband Lamont, without which this text would have never been completed. Final thanks goes to my son Desmond for being a reminder of why it is important to strive to create a better future.

INTRODUCTION

In a 1963 interview, Malcolm X stridently proclaimed, "Christ wasn't white. Christ was a black man."[1] Some thirty years later, especially with the emergence of the Afrocentric movement in the Black community, many Black scholars and church leaders are vociferously repeating Malcolm's proclamation.[2] Black biblical scholar Cain Hope Felder has sharply pointed out that "the sweet little Jesus boy of the Negro spiritual was, in fact, quite Black."[3] Various Black church leaders have urged Black churches to destroy images of Christ with White skin and features, and to replace them with images of a Christ with Black skin and features.[4] This, they claim, will help to nurture the kind of Black self-esteem needed to mitigate the murderous/suicidal self-hate that is apparently present in various segments of the Black community.

Although Jesus' ethnicity and dark-skinned complexion are certainly important aspects of Christ's blackness, to call Christ Black points to more than simply ancestry or biological characteristics. Throughout Black religious history, the Blackness of Christ has had significant theological implications. My own understanding of the importance of Christ's blackness began with my appreciation of Christ's presence in my maternal grandmother's life.

My memories of my grandmother (whom my sisters, brother, and I affectionately called Mama) are still very vivid. She was a hardworking woman who carried the burden of supporting herself and her family. She got up daily, even when she did not feel like it, to run an elevator in the local postoffice. She returned home from work each evening to take care of my grandfather (her second husband) who suffered from multiple health problems. The daily struggle to "make it" was not new to my grand-

1

mother; it had become her way of life since the death of her first husband left her at the young age of eighteen with a small child (my mother) to rear. The picture I have always had of Mama Dorsey is of a poor, Black woman, without formal education, doing what she could to make it with few material resources for survival.

I admired Mama because of her determination to survive. Despite the enormous difficulties involved in trying to do so, she never complained. She continued to smile and always made our frequent visits with her very pleasant. I often wondered how she did it. After watching her in church, seeing how she never failed to get on her knees to pray before going to bed, and noticing her Bible always opened to the twenty-third psalm, I had no doubt that it was because of her faith in the God of Jesus Christ that she could "keep going day in and day out."

When Mama sat on her front porch at night after everyone was asleep, with a cup of coffee and a bowl of rice, relaxing after a long day, I often got out of bed to sit with her. As I sat there with my head in her lap, I instinctively knew that she was thanking Jesus for bringing her safely to another night on the front porch.

Reflecting back on my grandmother's faith, I now realize that she must have trusted that the Christ she prayed to had a special appreciation of her condition. This was a Christ who seemingly identified with a poor Black woman in her day-to-day struggle just to make it. Mama was certain that this Christ cared about the trials and tribulations of an ordinary Black woman. Christ empowered her to get through each day with dignity.

As I learned more about the faith that supported Black people in their struggle through slavery and the many other trials of White racism, I discovered that my grandmother's faith was not unique. The Black Christian experience has been one in which Black people have consistently confirmed the presence of a sustaining and liberating Christ in their lives. This Christ reflects Black people's strident no to any notion that the God of Jesus Christ put them on earth to be chattel, "strange fruit" in Southern trees, or anything less than full human persons. This sustaining and liberating Christ of Black faith represents God's urgent movement in human history to set Black captives free from the demons of White racism.

Whether she consciously thought about it or not, my grand-mother's faith—a faith shared by many other Black people—suggested something about the Blackness of Christ. It affirmed that Christ was Black in that Christ identified with the Black struggle against the tyrannies of a White racist society.

My next encounter with the Black Christ came through the study of James Cone's book, *A Black Theology of Liberation*[5] and other Black theological texts. Indeed, no persons to date have more fully explored the meaning of Christ's Blackness than have Black theologians. They have attempted to define the Black Christ in terms of both Christ's color as well as relationship to Black people's struggle. At the same time, their careful exami-nations of what it means for Christ to be Black have revealed the limitations of the Black Christ for a Black community strug-gling against more than just White racism. Many of these limi-tations are evidenced in Black churches' responses to the various challenges of a changing Black community.

Cornel West aptly points out that one of the "distinctive fea-tures" of Black Christianity "has been its capacity to make vis-ible and potent its progressive prophetic pole."[6] He explains:

Nat Turner, Denmark Vesey, and Gabriel Prosser—Chris-tian preachers who led slave insurrections in the nine-teenth century—signify in dramatic fashion the crucial role of the black church in the Afro-American struggle for free-dom. . . . In short, the African appropriation of Christianity under conditions of slavery in the USA, the land of free-dom and opportunity in the eyes of many, produces a unique version of Christianity with strong prophetic ten-dencies.[7]

At the center of this prophetic tradition has been the Black Christian understanding of Jesus Christ. As earlier suggested, they have understood that Christ was against White racism and for Black freedom. This Christ has empowered Black Christians and Black churches to be prophetic in relation to issues of race in America. The Black church has historically been in the forefront of Black people's fight for life and liberation against the tyrannies of White racial oppression. Yet, as has become evident today, many Black churches have appeared ill prepared to respond to concerns that go beyond race. Black youth have found the churches' message virtually irrelevant as they have confronted the challenges of a drug culture, sex, and an uncertain future. Black churches have been impotent in responding to the AIDS crisis, which has fostered discrimination of gay and lesbian persons. Most significantly, Black churches and Black church denominations have been unable to empower and nurture more than one half of its own constituency, Black women. Black churches have been notorious in their refusal to recognize women's calls to a full-fledged ordained ministry. Women have been denied access to pulpits and decision-making roles in the Black church. This church has all too often been described as one of the last bastions of sexism.

Why is it that a significant number of Black churches have been incapable of responding to issues involving class, gender, and sexual oppression? Why has the Black church community appeared incapable of a prophetic ministry beyond matters of race?

In part, the Black church's inability to respond to the complex issues of class, gender, and sexuality is tied to the way in which Christ's Blackness has been defined. First, the Blackness of Christ in the Black church community has had more to do with Christ's commitment to Black freedom than to Christ's appearance. As contemporary advocates for the Black Christ have made clear, far too many Black churches speak of the Christ who is against White racism while still displaying images of White male Christs in their buildings and pulpits. One of the most visible images in the sanctuary of the recently built National Baptist Headquarters (Nashville, Tennessee) is that of a White Christ.

The Black church leaders who want to take down images of White Christs in their churches are right: a blond-haired, blue-eyed Christ does not empower or nurture self-esteem for Black people. This Christ is not a reflection of who they are as a people. It serves to remind many Black people of those who have come to personify White racism. A White Christ looks too much like the enemy in a White racist society. Moreover, such an image is not inviting to Black youth who are in need of developing positive self-images. A White Christ cannot provide them with the kind of role model they need to feel good about who they are as Black men and women. In essence, the centrality of White Christs in Black churches potentially alienates significant segments of the Black community. A story from the childhood of the late Black tennis star Arthur Ashe illustrates the point:

> Every Sunday, Arthur Jr. had to go to church, either to First Presbyterian or Westwood Baptist, where his parents had met and where he would look up at a picture of Christ with blond hair and blue eyes and wonder if God was on his side.[8]

Second, regardless of the images displayed throughout Black churches, the Christ of Black faith is committed to the liberation of Black people from White racism. In this respect, as suggested earlier, Christ can be understood as Black. But this "Black Christ" draws attention to only one dimension of Black oppression. Such a Christ challenges Black churches to be prophetic in relation to issues of race, but has little impact beyond that. Black churches then become captive to their history in relation to the race struggle as well as captive to their limited understanding of Christ's presence.

What does all this mean in relation to the significance and vitality of the Black Christ, even as new voices are proclaiming Christ's Blackness? Fundamentally, a proper understanding of the Black Christ ought to refer to both Christ's physical appearance and to Christ's relationship to the Black freedom struggle. The Blackness of Christ then is not determined by images or actions alone. A defining assumption of this book is that to call Christ "Black" suggests something about both Christ's appearance and actions. Such a Christ signifies my grandmother's faith that Christ is intimately involved in the Black struggle "to make do and do better," as well as the need for Black people to see themselves in Christ.

Yet in order for the Black Christ to be effective and prophetic in relationship to the contemporary Black quest for freedom, it must have meaning in relation to issues beyond White racism. At the very least, more has to be said about the Blackness of Christ than has historically been said, which frees it from the narrow confines of White racism. This book is an attempt to say more.

WHO IS THE BLACK CHRIST?

The first part of this book explores the meaning of the Black Christ to date. The underlying assumption is that although certain facets of the Black Christ have emerged throughout history—that is, skin color or existential commitment—the Black Christ did not come to theological fruition until the birth of Black theology in the United States. It was with Black theology that what Christ looked like, as well as how Christ acted came together to define Christ's Blackness. Chapter 1 examines what has been said about Christ in slavery, early Black nationalist thought, and early Black literature that ultimately culminated into the Black theological definition of Christ as Black. These three aspects of Black history and culture are examined because they each provide a framework for appreciating the significance of claiming Christ as Black. The analysis of what was said about Christ in slavery, Black nationalism, and Black literature is not meant to be exhaustive, even as it applies to the Black Christ. The intent of this discussion is to illuminate the various aspects of what it means to call Christ Black.

Black theology, and hence the Black Christ, was an immediate response to the 1960s civil rights/Black Power movement. As Gayraud Wilmore poignantly comments, "Black Theology was formulated by Christian activists in response to events which had the unmistakable sign that God is saying and doing something about Black people in White America."[9]

Chapter 2 will attempt to capture the dynamics of the civil rights/Black Power era, which forced the Black Christ to come to theological fruition. It will do this primarily by focusing on the theological challenges set forth by the work and thought of Martin Luther King, Jr., and Malcolm X. These two men are seen as the catalyst that forced Black theologians to say something definite about Christ's relationship to a Black people fighting for life, dignity, and freedom.

Chapter 3 examines three distinct models of the Black Christ that emerged in Black theology. It focuses on the interpretations of Albert Cleage, James Cone, and J. Deotis Roberts of what it means for Christ to be Black. The focus on these three theologians is not meant to suggest that they provide the only models for understanding Christ's Blackness, or that they were the only Black theologians to say something about who Christ was for a Black people in struggle. Other theologians from that period — such as Gayraud Wilmore, Major Jones, and William Eichleberger — all had something to say about the meaning of Christ for Black people.[10] This book focuses on these three theologians because they represent the diverse range of thought concerning Christ's Blackness, and they provide the most developed theological understandings. This chapter is written to provide those who may not be familiar with what these theologians have said about Christ a concise and clear understanding of their perspectives. For those who are more familiar with the development of the Black Christ in theological literature, this chapter hopes to provide a new way of ordering what Cleage, Cone, and Roberts had to say in relation to each other.

To maintain the integrity of the time period when the Black Christ emerged, the language used by the contributors to its development, including the language of the Black theologians, will be maintained. Some of their language reflects a pre-Black consciousness spirit when it refers to Black people as *Negro*. In addition, the language of this period reveals a general lack of consciousness concerning women's unique experience and perception of God. It should also be noted that since the major developers of early Black theology were men, when I speak of *Black theologians*, I am referring only to men.

IS THE BLACK CHRIST ENOUGH?

The second part of this book explores the potential and limitations of the Black Christ, and proposes what more must be said about the Blackness of Christ. Chapter 4 critically evaluates each interpretation of the Black Christ in relationship to two questions: Do the particular theological interpretations adequately represent what it means for Christ to be Black? Does the Black Christ adequately point to Christ's significance and presence within the contemporary Black community? Black women's experience of struggle will be the vantage point from which the latter question will be addressed.

Chapter 5 attempts to say something more about the Blackness of Christ. It puts forth an understanding of the Black Christ more reflective of Christ's significance for Black men and women. This discussion focuses specifically on a *womanist* portrayal of the Black Christ. Given the historically prophetic significance of the Black church in the Black struggle, and the centrality of Christ in that church, special attention will be given to the implications of a womanist understanding of Christ for the Black church.

I do not intend to provide a definitive answer concerning Christ's meaning for Black people as they struggle for a better life. My hope is that in telling the story of the Black Christ from a womanist perspective, I can contribute in moving us all closer to appreciating Christ's presence in Black lives as well as understanding the radical challenge that Christ gives to all Christians.

Chapter 1

THE ROOTS OF THE BLACK CHRIST

In March 1969 a picture of a kinky-haired, broad-nosed Black Christ was on the cover of *Ebony* magazine.[1]

This cover reflected a new era in Black America — the Black consciousness era. This was an era when a determined segment of the Black community had declared war on Whiteness. Freedom-fighting young Black men and women led Black people to a renewed sense of self-awareness, self-determination, and Black pride.

From the political arena to the religious arena, these freedom fighters demanded new symbols that would be uncompromising representations of a contagious spirit of Black identity. They called for secular and sacred images that would unambiguously assert the Black community's independence from White control and authority. At a time when Black people were "flamingly assertive and proud," the challenge to Christianity was clear: the White Christ and its religion had to go!

The young freedom fighters let it be known that there was no room in the Black community for a Christ who revealed utter contempt for Black life. They loathed the Christ who supported the ravage of Africa, fostered the bondage of Black people, stood silently by during the rapes of Black women, and shamed Black people "by his pigmentation so obviously not [their] own."[2] Vincent Harding captured the sentiments of these young people when he wrote, "the angry children of Malcolm X shout fiercely: 'To hell with you [White people] and your Christ!' "[3]

What was going on? What was this battle between the two

9

Christs all about? Who was the White Christ? Who was the Black Christ? What did they have to do with each other? What did they have to do with Jesus? What did they have to do with the Black struggle for freedom?

These are some of the questions that need to be answered if we are to understand Black theologians' declaration that "Christ is Black." This chapter will begin to answer these questions by providing the historical background to the emergence of the Black Christ within the contemporary Black theological movement.

To reiterate, a comprehensive understanding of the Black Christ must at least involve both Christ's color and relationship to the Black struggle for freedom. Although such an understanding of Christ did not emerge until Black theology, different aspects of Christ's Blackness were highlighted from time to time throughout Black history. In this regard, the roots of the Black Christ can be traced to the "sacred time" of slavery.[4] During slavery the Black Christ emerged in contradistinction to the oppressive White Christ. The White Christ was the center of slaveholding Christianity, while the Black Christ was the center of slave Christianity. The terms "slaveholding Christianity" and "slave Christianity" are not used to convey that either all slaveholders or all slaves possessed the same religious beliefs. Instead, they signify that a number of slaveholders found a way to participate in the business of slavery without denouncing their Christian faith. Similarly, a number of slaves found a way to fight for freedom without surrendering their Christianity. As slaveholding Christianity and slave Christianity emerged and confronted each other, so too did the White and Black Christs.

SLAVEHOLDING CHRISTIANITY AND THE WHITE CHRIST

Slavery in the American colonies was a part of a wider ideological structure, which presupposed that hierarchal relationships between human beings were divinely ordered. This belief system began with the notion that human beings were created unequal (despite later refutation of this in the Declaration of Independence). Certain biological and social realities were considered representative of superior human qualities, while certain others were considered representative of inferior human qualities. According to this perspective, it was the divinely sanctioned duty of those persons presumed superior to "care" for and govern those persons presumed inferior.

As imperialistically minded Europeans began to encounter the unique customs and culture of African people, they decided that dark skin was an unquestionable mark of inferiority. This erroneous notion was soon supported by various segments of the "scientific" and political community. A prominent eighteenth-century naturalist Carolus Linnaeus developed a human classification chart that affirmed theories of Black inferiority. On his chart he described Europeans as "White, Sanguine, Brawny. . . . Gentle acute, inventive. . . . Governed by customs." But he described Africans as "Black, Phlegmatic, Relaxed . . . Crafty, indolent. . . . Governed by Caprice."[5] Eminent eighteenth-century American physicians like Benjamin Rush speculated that the "color of Negroes" was a disease.

Political leaders such as Thomas Jefferson declared:

The first difference which strikes us is that of colour . . . the difference is fixed in nature, and is as real as if its seat and cause were better known to us. And is this difference of no importance? Is it not the foundation of a greater or less share of beauty in the two races? Are not the fine mixtures of red and white, the expressions of every passion by greater or less suffusions of colour in the one, preferable to that eternal monotony, which reigns in the countenances, that immoveable veil of black which covers all the emotions of the other race?[6]

The case for African inferiority seemed clear. Members of the White ruling class considered themselves superior to African people. They were certain that they were destined to be masters, while the dark-skinned Africans were destined to be slaves. One proslavery advocate explained:

The Order that God hath set in the World, who hath Ordained different degrees and orders of men . . . some to be Low and Despicable; some to be Monarchs, Kings,

Princes and Governors, Masters and Commanders, others to be Subjects, and to be Commanded . . . yea, some to be born Slaves, and so to remain during their lives.[7]

Yet, in spite of their apparent beliefs in divinely sanctioned human inequality, many Christian slaveholders faced some potential contradictions. How could they espouse Christian justice and freedom while participating in the bondage of other human beings? Were they committing a grievous sin? Some believed they were, as exemplified by the prayer of one slaveholding woman:

Oh my father, from the distressing task of regulating the conduct of my fellow-creatures in bondage, I turn and rest my weary soul on thy parental bosom. . . . My soul hath felt the awful weight of sin, so as to despair in agony—so as to desire that I had never had being. Oh God! then— then I felt the importance of a mediator, not only to *intercede* but to *suffer* under the burden of guilt.[8]

Others from the slaveholding class did not believe that slavery was a sin. They developed a religious apology for the chattel system—that of slaveholding Christianity. The White Christ was the center of this religion. The White Christ characteristically allowed for (1) the justification of slavery, (2) Christians to be slaves, and (3) the compatibility of Christianity with the extreme cruelty of slavery.

Justification of Slavery

Almost from the very beginning of the American slave trade, many slaveholders justified stealing Africans from their homeland—and enslaving them—with claims that they were introducing the "African heathens" to Jesus Christ. They reasoned that they were rescuing Africans from an ignominious life as pagans. These slaveholders rationalized that the benefit the slaves received from Christianization—that is, the assurance of salvation—far outweighed the brutality of slavery. As one proslaver argued:

The condition of the slaves is far better than that of the Africans from among whom they have been brought. Instead of debased savages, they are, to a considerable extent, civilized, enlightened and christianized.[9]

An antebellum philosopher put it this way:

So it will be found that [God] permitted the introduction of the pagan African into this country, that he might be ... redeemed by the genius of the gospel, and returned to bless his kindred and his country. Thus all Africa shall, sooner or later, share the blessings of civilization and religion.[10]

This emphasis on introducing people, particularly Africans, to Jesus Christ is one of the marks of an interpretation of Christianity with the White Christ at its core.

The White Christ is grounded in an understanding of Christianity suggesting that Jesus of Nazareth was Christ, or the Messiah, because God was made flesh in him. The incarnation itself is considered the decisive feature of Christianity. That God became human is the essential fact in what it means for Jesus to be Christ. It is God's act that is important to who Jesus is. What Jesus did on earth has little if anything to do with what it means for him to be Christ. His ministry to the poor and oppressed is virtually inconsequential to this interpretation of Christianity. While this emphasis on God's becoming incarnate in Jesus has several implications for Christians and their salvation, the following are especially important to understanding the significance of the White Christ for slaveholding Christianity.

First, little is required of humans in order to receive salvation. Christians are the passive recipients of God's grace. If persons believe that God has become "human" in Jesus, and thus Jesus is Christ, then they do not have to be anxious about their salvation. To believe God's act in Jesus is to become convinced that through that act salvation has been secured. With salvation guaranteed through belief, White people could be slaveholders *and* Christian without guilt or fear about the state of their soul.

Second, in order for humans to benefit from God's saving act, they must have knowledge of Jesus as the divine/human encounter. Slavery supposedly provided the opportunity for Africans to attain this salvific knowledge. Apparently, to the minds of many slaveholders, enslavement was the only means Africans had for learning anything about Jesus.

In general, an interpretation of Christianity that focuses on God's coming from heaven and becoming incarnate in Jesus, while sacrificing Jesus' ministry, unleashes the possibility for the emergence of the White Christ. Undergirded with such an understanding of Christianity, slaveholders were free to develop a notion of Christ that justified the enslavement of Africans. And so they did. It was the White Christ, as the center of slaveholding Christianity, that allowed White slaveholders to engage in Black slavery with religious impunity.

Christianization of the Slaves

Though slavery was justified as a means for the African "heathen" to be saved, Christianization of the slaves was a slow process. Before the late eighteenth and nineteenth centuries, the number of slaves converted to Christianity was negligible. Slaveholders' resistance to the idea of Christianizing the slaves was a major barrier. Some slaveholders were concerned that Christianity would make their slaves recalcitrant and difficult to control. Others were concerned about the "legally vague but widely believed" notion that if the slaves were baptized, they would have to be emancipated.[11]

The major barrier to Christianizing the slaves was the slaveholders' fears that the freedom that Jesus offered the oppressed during his own time, and the egalitarian themes present throughout the New Testament, might make the slaves think that they should be free and equal to the White population.[12] Historian Albert Raboteau explains:

> The danger beneath the arguments for slave conversion which many masters feared was the egalitarianism implicit in Christianity. The most serious obstacle to the missionary's access to the slaves was the slaveholder's vague awareness that a Christian slave would have some claim

to fellowship, a claim that threatened the security of the master-slave hierarchy.[13]

The White Christ was the answer to this threat. This Christ gained stature in slaveholding Christianity as proslavery evangelists continued to support the idea that Jesus' liberating ministry was irrelevant to the Christian religion. They did this by first highlighting Old Testament scriptures, which apparently supported human bondage. For instance, they frequently quoted from the story of Ham (Genesis 9:25) and the Leviticus code (Leviticus 25:44–46).

Second, because the New Testament Gospels did not speak directly for or against slavery, proslavery evangelists argued that what was in the Old Testament was "authoritative in the Christian era unless it was abrogated in the New Testament."[14] Ignoring Jesus' liberating ministry to the oppressed as well as his commitment to "set the captives free," apologists for slavery argued that if Jesus had considered slavery a sin, he would have spoken directly against it. One proslavery minister made his case for slavery this way:

> Our Lord repeatedly spoke of slaves, especially in several of his parables, without the slightest intimation that he condemned slavery, and in such a way as plainly showed that he considered it lawful. . . .
> We are told, Matt. 8:23–35, that a Centurion came to Jesus beseeching him to heal his sick servant. . . . If the holding of slaves had been sinful, Jesus would, we doubt not, have so informed [the Centurion].[15]

The White Christ is, thus, predicated upon an understanding of Jesus that disregards what he did do — that is, minister to the poor and oppressed — yet accents what he did not — that is, speak directly against slavery.

Finally, while proslavery evangelists had to rely upon the lack of antislavery statements when utilizing the New Testament Gospels to justify their position, they had what they considered direct support for slavery from the New Testament epistles. Historian H. Shelton Smith observed:

Defenders of human bondage felt much more at home in the letters of Paul than they did in the teachings of Jesus, because those documents contained specific instructions on the duties of masters and slaves. In fact, virtually every proslavery tract of any consequence explored the Pauline epistles far more exhaustively than any other portion of the New Testament.[16]

One ex-slave witnessed to the frequency with which she would hear Ephesians preached: "[The white preacher] preached, 'you must obey your masters and be good servants.' That is the greater part of the sermon, when they preach to colored folks."[17]

The direct attention given to slavery in the epistles notwithstanding, slaveholding evangelists' focus on the epistles — as opposed to the Gospels — is consistent with the religion of the White Christ. The Gospels are unimportant, since they concentrate on Jesus' liberating activity in human history. The epistles are important, because they stress knowledge of and belief in Jesus Christ as essential for human salvation.

The practical outcome of this New Testament selectivity in understanding Jesus is that it provided proslavery evangelists a way to quell the fears of slaveholders. Evangelists were able to spiritualize the themes of Christian freedom and equality. They essentially reasoned that what Jesus did in human history was disconnected from the salvation that he offered. Subsequently, the salvation that he offered was unrelated to what took place in human history. Jesus' salvation had nothing to do with historical freedom. The slaves could be Christian without being freed. According to this version of Christianity, the only freedom Jesus offered was in "heaven" not on earth.

The Bishop of London put it this way:

Christianity, and the embracing of the Gospel does not make the least Alteration in Civil property, or in any of the Duties which belong to Civil Relations; but in all these Respects, it continues Persons just in the same State as it found them. The Freedom which Christianity gives, is a Freedom from the Bondage of Sin and Satan, and from the Dominion of Men's Lust and Passions and inordinate

Desires; but as to their outward Condition, whatever that was before, whether bond or free, their being baptized and becoming Christians, makes no matter of Change in it.[18]

To assure that the slaves understood baptism was not synonymous with earthly freedom, many White evangelists had slaves consent to declarations like the following:

You declare in the presence of God and before this Congregation that you do not ask for the Holy Baptism out of any design to free yourself from the Duty and Obedience you owe to your Master while you live, but meerly [sic] for the good of your Soul and to partake of the Graces and Blessings promised to the Members of the Church of Jesus Christ.[19]

Again, with an interpretation of Christianity and a reading of the Bible that trivializes Jesus' earthly ministry, the White Christ can flourish. It did so in slaveholding Christianity. This Christ allowed for White enslavers to be Christians, and for Black Christians to be slaves.

Christianity and Cruelty

In addition to permitting a justification for slavery, and a means for evangelizing slaves without disrupting the slaveocracy, the White Christ is implicated in the slaveholders' unwillingness to acknowledge the contradiction between Christianity and the cruelty of slavery. Although some antebellum evangelists argued that the Christian slaveholder was more "benevolent" toward slaves than the non-Christian slaveholder, from many slaves' points of view this claim was more rhetoric than reality. To be sure, there were some "converted" slaveholders who occasionally reduced their slaves' workloads so that the slaves could attend religious instruction. The slaveholders' conversions, however, rarely meant more humane treatment of their human chattel. In fact, slave testimony suggests that the Christian slaveholder was just as cruel, if not more so, than the non-Christian slaveholder. Ex-slave Susan Bogg remembered:

I didn't see any difference between the slaveholders who had religion and those who had not. . . . Why the man that baptized me had a colored woman tied up in his yard to whip when he got home, that very Sunday and her mother belonged to that same church. We had to sit and hear him preach. . . . And he had her tied up and whipped. That was our preacher![20]

Another ex-slave said, "The professed Christians at [sic] the South didn't treat their slaves any better than other people, nor so well. I'd rather live with a cardplayer and a drunkard than with a Christian."[21] Frederick Douglass's feelings best convey the sentiments of many slaves:

Were I to be again reduced to the chains of slavery, next to the enslavement, I should regard being the slave of a religious master the greatest calamity that could befall me. For of all slaveholders with whom I have ever met, religious slaveholders are the worst. I have ever found them the meanest and basest, more cruel and cowardly, of all others.[22]

What is it about slaveholding Christianity that allows for brutal slaveholders? Why does the Christian slaveholder often seem more cruel than the non-Christian slaveholder? What prevents Christian slaveholders from acknowledging the contradiction between their hideous treatment of their slaves and their belief in Jesus Christ?

The answer to the above questions is the White Christ. To reiterate, the White Christ is based on an understanding of Jesus in which his liberating ministry is of little significance. Salvation is guaranteed because God is incarnate in him. The general consequences of this understanding are twofold.

First, after a person is converted to belief in Jesus as Christ, his or her salvation is automatic; he or she no longer has to be anxious about it. This assurance, found in conversion, apparently freed many slaveholders to do whatever they deemed necessary to keep their slaves under control. Fear for their own salvation no longer regulated their behavior toward their slaves — if it did before.

Second, because Jesus' ministry is ignored, his liberating actions do not become a standard for Christian actions. The emphasis is placed on God's act in Jesus — not on human actions in response to Jesus' liberating activity. The Christian feels no obligation to treat others, especially the oppressed, the way Jesus treated them. Again, enslavers are free to be as cruel as they want toward a slave, while at the same time being assured salvation. The religion of the White Christ places few demands on persons concerning how they should live their life in relation to others.

Slaveholding Christianity clearly reveals a major shortcoming of an interpretation of Christianity that emphasizes the incarnation at the expense of Jesus' earthly ministry. It can lead to an understanding of Christ that supports an unjust status quo. In America it produced the White Christ — the Christ whom "the angry children of Malcolm X" railed against. This Christ allowed for the maintenance of an oppressive social-economic system and freed the White ruling class to act in ways that benefited them — without fear for their salvation. Specifically, the White Christ provided for the religious justification of the chattle system, eliminated reservations about holding Christians as slaves, and obscured the tensions between Christianity and the cruelty of slavery. Frederick Douglass aptly described the religion of the White Christ when he said:

[T]he religion of the south is a mere covering for the most horrid crimes — a justifier of the most appalling barbarity — a sanctifier of the most hateful frauds — and a dark shelter under which the darkest, foulest, grossest, and most infernal deeds of slaveholders find the strongest protection.[23]

If slaveholding Christianity and the White Christ are the only way in which Christianity and Jesus' significance can be understood, then the refrain, "to hell with White people and their Christ," is not enough. Freedom-seeking Black people would have to shout "To hell with Christianity and its Jesus." Fortunately Black slaves provided another understanding of Christianity and its Jesus.

SLAVE CHRISTIANITY AND THE BLACK CHRIST

Slaveholders tried to convince slaves to accept the slaveholding version of Christianity. While some slaves "found meaning in the message spread by [slaveholding] missionaries, accepted it on faith and tried their best to incorporate it in their lives," many others rejected it.[24] Those who rejected it may have attended worship services held by slaveholding preachers, and listened patiently to the preacher's message; but they did not consider these services "real church," nor did they think the preacher's message was Christian. Ex-slave Charlie Van Dyke explained: "Church was what they called it but all that preacher talked about was for us slaves to obey our masters and not to lie and steal. Nothing about Jesus was ever said."[25]

If the slaveholder was concerned with whether he or she could own slaves and yet be saved, then the slave was concerned with whether he or she could fight for freedom and yet remain Christian. The Christian slaves wanted to know if Jesus was for or against freedom from human bondage. The slaveholding version of Christianity did its best to denounce any notions that Jesus and historical freedom were compatible.

Disgusted by slaveholding Christianity and its White Christ, some slaves held clandestine services—away from the watchful eyes of their masters and mistresses—where they had "real church" and heard what they considered *Christian* preaching. "In the secrecy of the quarters or the seclusion of the brush arbors ('hush harbors') the slaves made Christianity truly their own."[26] These hidden services nurtured slave Christianity. The Black Christ was center of this religion. The Black Christ characteristically (1) reflected an intimate relationship between Jesus and the slaves, (2) radicalized the slaves to fight for their freedom, and (3) illuminated the contradiction between Christianity and the cruelty of slavery.

Jesus and the Slaves

Slave Christianity did not focus on the relationship between Jesus and God as did slaveholding Christianity. The significance

of Jesus for the slaves had little to do with God becoming incarnate in him. Jesus' meaning had more to do with what Jesus did
in their lives. Jesus was a living being with whom the slaves had
an intimate relationship. Refrains like "Jesus is my bosom
friend," "He will be wid us Jesus,/Be wid us to the end," and
"a little talk with Jesus Makes it right," echo through slave
songs. To the slaves, Jesus was a trusted companion who understood their pain, sufferings, and sorrows.

What allowed slaves to develop such a special relationship
with Jesus? Why were they so confident that Jesus was their
friend and confidant — especially when the image that the slaveholders presented to them of Jesus suggested the opposite?

Jesus' significance for the slaves was based upon an interpretation of Christianity that stressed the centrality of Jesus' ministry and relationship to the oppressed during his own time. The
slaves were drawn, for instance, to Luke's birth narrative. For
them this narrative established Jesus' bond with the outcast and
downtrodden at the very beginning of his life. It told that Jesus
was born in a manger, because there was no room for him in
the inn. Luke's report of the circumstances into which Jesus was
born seemingly assured the slaves that Jesus understood their
experience of rejection. They sang:

> Poor little Jesus boy
> Made him to be born in a manger
> World treated him so mean
> Treats me mean too.[27]

The crucifixion was, however, the event that most clearly
demonstrated to the slaves Jesus' solidarity with them. It forged
an inextricable bond between the two. Through the cross, Jesus'
suffering and the slaves' suffering became one. The slaves sang,
"Were you there when they crucified my Lord?," passionately
implying that they were there. The slave's identification with
Jesus' suffering on the cross was evidenced in the way they
poignantly pictured the details of his crucifixion:

> Oh, dey whupped him up de hill, up de hill, up de
> hill,

Oh, dey whupped him up de hill, an' he never said
　a mumbalin word,
Oh, dey whupped him up de hill, an' he never said
　a mumbalin word,
He jes' hung down his head an' he cried. . . .

Oh, dey crowned him wid a thorny crown . . .

Well, dey nailed him to de cross, to de cross, to de
　cross.[28]

Recognizing the slaves' empathy with Jesus' crucifixion, Howard
Thurman says:

In the spirituals the death of Jesus took on a deep and
personal poignancy. It was not merely the death of a man
or a God. . . . The suffering of Jesus on the cross was something more. He suffered, He died, but not alone—they
were with Him. They knew that he suffered; it was a cry
of the heart that found response and an echo in their own
woes.[29]

Essentially, through the cross the slaves' experience and
Jesus' experience converged. The suffering of slavery and the
suffering of the cross were synonymous. The crucifixion confirmed to slaves that they were one with Jesus, and more importantly, that Jesus was one with them. James Cone explains:

Through the blood of slavery, they transcended the limitations of space and time. Jesus' time became their time,
and they encounterd a new historical existence. Through
the experience of being slaves, they encountered the theological significance of Jesus' death: through the crucifixion, Jesus makes an unqualified identification with the
poor and the helpless and takes their pain upon himself.[30]

To be sure, the slaves' African religious heritage influenced
their acceptance and interpretation of the Christian cross. A
cross was a familiar symbol in many African religions. It sym-

bolized the cycle of life and death. It also pointed to the profound ongoing relationship between the living and the dead, the African and his or her ancestors.[31] The African cross symbol undoubtedly made it easier for African slaves to accept the Christian cross. The intimate relationship between the living and the dead, which the African cross pointed to, more than likely influenced the slaves' development of a special relationship with Jesus, the crucified one. Whatever the underlying factors, Jesus' cross allowed slaves to be certain that Jesus understood what it meant to be a slave and that he was one with them in their struggle to survive.

The slaves were also sure that Jesus would take care of their every need. They sang:

> O Lord, I'm hungry
> I want to be fed,
> O Lord, I'm hungry
> I want to be fed,
> O feed me Jesus feed me,
> Feed me all my days.

> O Lord, I'm naked
> I want to be clothed,
> O Lord, I'm naked
> I want to be clothed,
> O clothe me Jesus clothe me
> Clothe me all my days.[32]

This assurance was again based on the slaves' knowledge of Jesus' earthly ministry. They testified in song:

> Jesus make de dumb to speak.
> Jesus make de cripple walk.
> Jesus give de blind his sight.
> Jesus do most anything.[33]

They reasoned that if Jesus helped the oppressed of his own time, he would surely do the same for them:

Lord help the po' and the needy,
In this lan' . . .
In this great getting up morning we shall face another
        sun,
Lord help the po' and the needy,
In this lan', In this lan' . . .
Lord help the widows and the orphans, In this
        lan' . . .
Lord help the motherless children, In this lan'.[34]

Fundamental to the slaves' belief that Jesus would meet their needs was the resurrection. The resurrection revealed that Jesus was not dead. The crucified one was the resurrected one—who was now acting in contemporary history.[35] The slaves gave witness: "Go and tell ev'rybody / Yes, Jesus is risen from the dead.[36]" An interpreter of slave songs, John Lovell, aptly observes, "Without a doubt . . . the really powerful Jesus of the spiritual works on earth, in this life, in the here and now, today and tomorrow."[37]

The resurrection also revealed that the death of the cross was not the last word—freedom was. Since slave Christianity viewed the cross and slavery as synonymous experiences, Jesus' deliverance from the death of the cross meant they would be delivered from the death of slavery. Black people testified in song that "Jesus Christ, He died for me, Jesus Christ He set me free."

The slaves forged an interpretation of Christianity that focused on Jesus' ministry to the oppressed, as well as the crucifixion and resurrection within the context of that ministry. Such an interpretation allows for the emergence of the Black Christ. And so it did with slave Christianity. The Black Christ was the presence of Jesus in slave lives. He was for the slave a fellow sufferer, a confidant, a provider, and a liberator.

Radicalization of the Slaves

Just as an emphasis on Jesus' ministry opened the slaves to an intimate relationship with Jesus, it also radicalized them to fight for their freedom. Contrary to slaveholding Christianity, slave Christianity did not thoroughly spiritualize the Christian concept of freedom. Instead, Christian freedom had secular and radical implications. Although there were some slaves who adopted slaveholding Christianity and its notion that the freedom that Jesus offered was attainable only in "heaven," for the many others who rejected and produced slave religion, the freedom that Jesus offered was a reality to be attained on earth.

Christianity did not make these slaves docile. It did not lead them to wait passively for a day of emancipation. Rather, it made them rebellious. It radicalized them to fight for their freedom. This is evidenced by the struggles such as those led by Gabriel Prosser, Denmark Vesey, Nat Turner, Sojourner Truth, and Harriet Tubman. These struggles were often supported with Christian themes. The slave's determination to be free was also expressed in song:

> O freedom! O freedom!
> O freedom over me!
> An' befo' I'd be a slave,
> I'll be buried in my grave,
> An' go home to my Lord an' be free.[38]

Granted, the meaning of freedom—especially in slave songs —was occasionally ambiguous.[39] Sometimes it did point to a freedom beyond this world.[40] However, the freedom that was hoped for in the "next world" was seldom totally divorced from the expectations of "this world." It was not completely spiritulized. The freedom of the other world impacted the slaves' world. It motivated them to continue the struggle to survive and be free, because they knew that their struggle was not in vain: "de udder worl' is not like dis."

The slaves' view of freedom was in great measure shaped by their interpretation of the biblical message. As slaveholding Christianity fostered a certain selectivity in interpreting the biblical message, so too did slave Christianity. Slaveholding Christianity avoided the Gospels because of their concentration on Jesus' ministry. It valued the epistles because of their emphases on attaining proper knowledge of Jesus and on obedience. Slave Christianity avoided Paul's epistles because of their lack of emphasis on historical liberation, as well as apparent sanctioning of slavery. It valued the Old Testament because of its focus on God's liberating acts in history.

Howard Thurman's story of why his grandmother never allowed him to read to her from Paul's epistles portrays one side of the slaves' biblical selectivity. He remembered his grandmother explaining to him:

> During the days of slavery . . . the master's minister would occasionally hold services for the slaves. . . . Always the white minister used as his text something from Paul. At least three times a year he used as a text: "Slaves, be obedient to them that are your masters . . . as unto Christ."
> . . . I promised my Maker that if I ever learned to read and if freedom ever came, I would not read that part of the Bible.[41]

The other side of the slaves' biblical selectivity is portrayed by their emphasis on God's acts in Israelite history. The world of the Old Testament shaped slave Christianity. What God did for people in the Old Testament, the slaves were sure God would do for them. The slaves sang:

> He delivered Daniel from de lion's den,
> Jonah from de belly ob de whale,
> And de Hebrew children from de fiery furnace,
> And why not every man?[42]

Identifying particularly with the Israelite slaves, Black slaves often sang songs about the exodus event, which expressed a certainty that God would deliver them as God delivered the Israelites:

> When the children were in bondage,
> They cried unto the Lord,
> To turn back Pharaoh's army,
> He turned back Pharaoh's army.
>
> When Pharaoh crossed the water,
> The waters came together,

And drowned ole Pharaoh's army,
Hallelu![43]

Raboteau explains the significance of the exodus event in slave religion this way:

The slaves believed that God had acted, was acting, and would continue to act within human history and within their own particular history as a peculiar people just as long ago he had acted on behalf of another chosen people, biblical Israel.[44]

That Daniel, Jonah, the Hebrew children, and the Israelites were all delivered in *this* world had additional importance in slave Christianity. These stories of deliverance shaped how the slaves interpreted Jesus' freedom. It was a divine freedom granted in this world. The slaves seemed to transform Jesus into the Old Testament hero, Moses. As Moses delivered the Israelites from bondage, Jesus would deliver the slaves. One observer of slave religion noted that Jesus Christ was considered "not so much in the light of a *spiritual* Deliverer, as that of a second Moses."[45]

In general, slave Christianity focused on the Old Testament stories of God's liberating acts in Israelite history. This focus provided slaves with the basis for interpreting the freedom Jesus offered. It was a freedom that could be achieved in this world. The Jesus that empowered the Black slaves to fight for their emancipation from the chains of White slavery, was the Black Christ. This Christ was the center of slave Christianity. Consequently, slave Christianity was not an otherworldly religion that led the slaves to be docile and obedient — as slaveholders hoped. Rather, it nurtured a rebellion against and resistance to dehumanizing slavery. Raboteau explains:

Slave religion had a this-worldly impact, not only in leading some slaves to acts of external rebellion, but also in helping slaves to assert and maintain a sense of personal value even of worth.[46]

The Contradiction between Christianity and the Cruelty of Slavery

In addition to reflecting Jesus' intimate relationship with the slaves and radicalizing them, the Black Christ is also implicated in the slaves' awareness of the contradiction between Christianity and the cruelty of slavery. Slaves saw a contradiction between being a Christian and being a slaveholder. Ex-slave Henry Bibb described the contradiction plainly when he wrote to his slavemaster, "you have no right to be a slaveholder. ... The religion which you profess forbids it. ... And the voice of God has ever been to break every yoke and to let the oppressed go free."[47] Those who confessed Jesus, yet wielded the whips and chains of slavery, were considered hypocrites. Frederick Douglass forcefully captured the hypocrisy that many slaves recognized:

> The slave auctioneer's bell and the churchgoing bell chime in with each other, and the bitter cries of the heartbroken slave are drowned in the religious shouts of his pious master. Revivals of religion and revivals in the slave-trade go hand in hand together. The slave prison and the church stand near each other. The clanking fetters and the rattling of chains in the prison, and the pious psalm and solemn prayer in the church, may be heard at the same time. ... But woe unto you, scribes and pharisees, hypocrites! ... even so ye also outwardly appear righteous unto men, but within ye are full of hypocrisy and iniquity.[48]

The understanding of Christian slaveholders as "hypocrites" is consistent with an interpretation of Christianity that does not bypass Jesus' ministry to the oppressed. Slave Christianity emphasized human responses in relation to Jesus' ministry. Jesus' actions toward the oppressed of his time become a standard for Christian behavior. A Christian is not free to treat the oppressed any way he or she wants. One who professes to be Christian is challenged to treat the oppressed the way Jesus treated them. According to slave Christianity, to enslave and brutalize others betrays the example that Jesus set and contradicts what it means to be Christian.

This emphasis on "right action" has implications for salvation. According to slaveholding Christianity, knowledge of God's act in Jesus was sufficient for salvation. Claiming to provide the slaves with this knowledge gave the slaveholders a rationale for the chattel system. According to slave Christianity, however, salvation was not linked necessarily to God's act of becoming incarnate in Jesus, but to what Jesus did in history on behalf of the downtrodden. He delivered them from the conditions that oppressed them. Salvation is tied to liberating activity, not to knowledge. In order for Christians to receive salvation, they must engage in liberating acts, not enslaving acts.

Ex-slave Henry Bibb made this clear when he said of the slaveholders' opportunity to be saved:

> The fellowship of no number of professing christians, however extended nor the solemn baptism and silent toleration of all the Reverend time serving ministers in creation, can make you really a christian, or dispense with the binding force of the Gospel of Jesus Christ as the rule of your life and practice; and whilst you continue in such an unhallowed course of conduct, your prayers, your solemn fasts and ordinances are an abomination to the Lord, from which he will turn his face away, in disgust and will not hear or look upon.[49]

The religion of the Black Christ circumscribes the way Christians ought to act toward others, especially toward the oppressed and downtrodden.

Slave religion clearly reveals a major strength of an approach to Christianity that emphasizes Jesus' earthly ministry. It can lead to an understanding of Jesus Christ as one who stands against an unjust status quo. From out of the slave quarters and the secrecy of the "hush harbors" it produced the Black Christ. This Christ was defined by opposition to an understanding of Jesus that supported the dehumanization of Black people. The Blackness of this Christ was most evident in this Christ's identification with the Black slaves and condemnation of the White slaveholders.

Specifically, the Black Christ stood with the Black slave in resistance to White bondage, radicalized them to fight for freedom, and clarified the compatibility between Christianity and human cruelty.

The Black Christ who was born in slavery made it possible for Black people to be Christian without worshiping a Christ that ravaged Africa, fostered slavery, and accepted the rapes of Black women. Yet it did not address the color issue. The Blackness of the slaves' Christ had to do with Christ's actions, not Christ's skin color. If Black Christians were not to be shamed by a Christ "whose pigmentation was so obviously not their own," something more had to be said about the Blackness of Christ.

The actual pigmentation of Christ was addressed as Black people overtly began to make the link between their biological characteristics, especially the color of their skin, and their social condition.

BLACK NATIONALISTS AND THE COLOR OF CHRIST

As early as the antebellum period, and throughout Black people's struggle against racial oppression, Black nationalist thinkers have been in the forefront in pointing to the color component of Black oppression. They have made it clear that in the United States Blackness is synonymous with inferiority, and hence unwarranted suffering.

In an effort to break the link between Blackness and inferiority, Black nationalist thinkers have promoted diverse programs that reflect concepts such as cultural chauvinism, race pride, economic solidarity, and back-to-Africa movements.[50] One of the most significant efforts to sever the bond between Blackness and inferiority has been the recognition of God and Christ as biologically Black. Identifying God and Christ as Black fosters Black people's self-esteem by allowing them to worship a God in their own image, and by signifying that Blackness is nothing to be detested. On the contrary, it is a color and condition that even the divine takes on. Black nationalists have made this point in various ways.

Robert Alexander Young calls Christ "Black" in his 1829 *Ethiopian Manifesto*. He begins this manifesto by arguing that enslavement of Blacks is against God's will. He says that Black people are created by God, just like White people; thus Whites have no right to prevent Black people from enjoying the freedom that God grants to all people. He writes:

> Am I, because I am a descendant of a mixed race of men whose shade hath stamped them with the hue of black, to deem myself less eligible to the attainment of the great gift allowed of God to man. . . . No, I am in myself a man . . . for as I was born free of the will alloted me of the freedom of God, so do I claim and purport to establish an alike universal freedom to every son and daughter descending from the black.[51]

Based on this claim that God intends for Blacks to be free, not enslaved, Young argues that God will send forth a messiah — born of a Black woman — who will liberate Black people "from the infernal state of bondage, under which [they] have been so long and so unjustly laboring."[52]

Young's version of the Black messiah echoes themes of slave Christianity by stressing that God is against slavery. But it does not reflect slave religion's stress on Jesus' unique relationship to the oppressed.

Henry McNeal Turner, in an 1898 speech, presents a model of the Black messiah that does not overtly link Blackness to God's opposition to oppression. He emphasizes, instead, the importance of Black people's ability to image God and Jesus in their own likeness:

> We have as much right biblically and otherwise to believe that God is a Negro, as you buckra, or white people have to believe that God is a fine looking symmetrical and ornamented white man. . . . Demented though we be, whenever we reach the conclusion that God or even that Jesus Christ,

while in the flesh, was a white man, we shall hang our gospel trumpet upon the willow and cease to preach.[53]

Later in the twentieth century, Marcus Garvey agreed with Turner that Black people had every right to envision God as Black. He reasoned:

We, as Negroes, have found a new ideal. Whilst our God has no color, yet it is human to see everything through one's own spectacles. . . . The God of Issac and the God of Jacob let Him exist for the race that believes in the God of Issac and the God of Jacob. We Negroes believe in the God of Ethiopia. . . . That is the God in whom we believe, but we shall worship Him through the spectacles of **Ethiopia**.[54]

Differing from Turner, however, Garvey argued that Jesus was actually Black. He said that as a Jew from the line of Jesse, Jesus had "Negro blood" running through his viens. Given this fact, he admonished a Black audience to "never admit that Jesus Christ was a white man."[55]

Although he did not relate it to Jesus' Blackness, Garvey, reminiscent of slave Christianity, used the cross to indicate the special relationship between Jesus and Black people. He said that Black people befriended Jesus when Simon the Cyrenian bore his cross to Calvary.[56]

EARLY BLACK LITERATURE AND THE BLACK CHRIST

The early twentieth century was an era in which Black literature also reflected an emphasis on the Black Christ. Langston Hughes, for instance, portrayed Christ as a Southern "nigger" in his poem entitled "Christ in Alabama." According to Hughes:

Christ is a nigger,
Beaten and black:
Oh, bare your back!

Mary is His mother:
Mammy of the South,
Silence your mouth.

God is His father:
White Master above
Grant Him your love.

Most holy bastard
Of the bleeding mouth,
Nigger Christ
On the cross
of the South.[57]

Countee Cullen, reflecting more of an existential struggle to
relate Christ to Black people, wrote a poem in 1928 entitled
"The Black Christ."[58] In his book *Color*, Cullen had already
published another poem, "Heritage," in which he communicated
the comfort that would derive from knowing that Christ, too,
was Black:

Ever at Thy glowing altar
Must my heart grow sick and falter,
Wishing He I served were black,
Thinking then it would not lack
Precedent of pain to guide it,
Let who would or might deride it,
Surely then this flesh would know
Yours had borne a kindred woe.[59]

Finally, John Henrik Clarke wrote a short story entitled "The
Boy Who Painted Christ Black." He relates the dramatic
account of a little boy who got in trouble with a White school
supervisor for painting a picture of a Black Christ. But the story
also tells of the heroic Black principal of the school who lost his
job for being bold enough to take a stand on the little boy's
behalf. In defending the little boy, the principal said:

I encouraged the boy in painting that picture. . . . And it
was with my permission that he brought the picture into

this school. I don't think the boy is so far wrong in painting Christ black. The artists of all other races have painted whatsoever God they worship to resemble themselves. I see no reason why we should be immune from that privilege. After all, Christ was born in that part of the world that had always been predominately populated by colored people. There is a strong possibility that he could have been a Negro.[60]

In summary, Black nationalists and Black literary artists have recognized the importance of Christ's being actually Black. Although calling Christ "Black" was a response to White racism, the conscious connection between Christ's Blackness and Christ's liberating activity was yet to come. Color was insignificant to the Black Christ as it emerged in slave Christianity while Christ's ministry was significant. Christ's ministry was not the primary concern in the development of the Black Christ in nationalism or Black literature, while color was.

When the Black Christ finally reached full development in Black theology, it reflected its roots in slave Christianity, Black nationalism, and Black literature. The events of the 1960s Civil Rights/Black Power movement forced Black theologians to define Christ's meaning in such a way that Christ opposed White racism *and* promoted pride in Blackness.

Chapter 2

THE BLACK STRUGGLE
AND THE BLACK CHRIST

The Black Christ was forced to maturity during the Civil Rights/Black Power movement with the advent of the Black consciousness era. This era officially began when SNCC chairperson Stokely Carmichael shouted the words "Black Power" during a 1966 protest march in the racist backwoods of Greenwood, Mississippi. As indicated earlier, this era was marked by Black people demanding, from the White community as well as from their own community, a respect for Blackness. This involved a respect not just for the color of their skins, but for their heritage, their music, their art, their culture in general. For instance, in 1968 the students of Howard University led a protest that closed the university for several days. This protest demanded that Howard's identification as a Black institution be reflected not just by its majority Black population, but also by a curriculum that focused on Black culture and heritage.

During this era of Black consciousness Black people all across America, especially young Black people, could be seen donning symbols of Blackness. They wore African dashikis, had African carved statues (Tikis) hanging from their necks, they wore large Afro-style haircuts, and carried in their back pockets Afro combs decorated with the Black Power symbol (a clenched Black fist). As Black youngsters strutted the streets clothed in "Blackness," they often shouted the words of a popular song during that era, "Say it loud, I'm Black and I'm Proud!"

But perhaps nothing signified this new ethos more than did the Black literature of this period. A Black asthetic movement had emerged. As creators of this movement, Black literary artists lifted up nationalist political themes and attempted to "give the fullest possible expression to the original styles of life, rhythms, images, sensibilities, musical patterns, and forms of language usage and idiom which Black people have developed as a part of the total Black experience in Africa and the Western world."[1] An excerpt from Imamu Amiri Baraka's (then Leroi Jones) poem "Sacred Chant for the Return of Black Spirit and Black Power" illustrates the type of Black literature that emerged as a part of this Black consciousness era:

> ohhh break love with white things.
> Ohhh, Ohhh break break break let it roll down.
>
> Let it kill, let it kill,
> let the thing you are destroy
> let it murder, and dance, and kill.
> Ohhh OhhhOhhh break
> the white thing.
> Let it dangle dead.
> Let it rot like nature needs.[2]

The spirit of Black consciousness, which had overtaken the Black community, was pregnant with religious and theological implications. Did Christianity support such a spirit? Could Jesus Christ have meaning for a people determined to be free and unabashedly proud of their Blackness? No two persons made these challenges to Christianity any clearer than did Martin Luther King, Jr., and Malcolm X. These two men were the catalysts who forced the Black Christ to come to theological fruition.

Confronting the White Christ in the rhetoric and actions of many White churchgoers, King carried forth the tradition of slave Christianity and the Black Christ as he assiduously linked Black freedom to the Christian gospel. Unmasking the evil of White racism, Malcolm X carried forth the nationalist tradition as he vociferously pointed to the absurdity of Black people worshiping a Christ that looked like their White oppressors. As Black theologians were forced by the social-political dynamics of the era to say something about Christ's Blackness, they would have to respond to the theological and religious claims of Martin and Malcolm. In an effort to appreciate the meaning of the Black Christ in Black theology, this chapter will explore the theological and religious underpinnings of Martin King's and Malcolm X's actions. It will also highlight the social-political dynamics unleashed by these two men, which forced Black theologians to speak.

MARTIN LUTHER KING, JR., AND THE BLACK CHRIST

The Reality of the White Christ

During the 1960s freedom struggle, the White Christ was an ever-present reality. Southern white clergy kept this Christ alive in their opposition to Martin King's civil rights involvement. Silence often characterized their opposition. Throughout much of the civil rights movement their voices were conspicuously absent. They did not voice a concern for racial justice. Just as slaveholders did not acknowledge a contradiction between Christianity and slavery, many southern white church leaders did not recognize a contradiction in being Christian yet silent in relation to Black oppression. Essentially, these church leaders did not believe that it was appropiate for Christian ministers to intervene in secular affairs. For them the minister's task was to "save souls."

To claim that a minister's responsibility is to save souls and not to become involved in social justice issues is consistent with the religion of the White Christ. The White Christ is based upon an understanding of Christianity that minimizes the significance of Jesus' ministry. The Christian is called to believe that Jesus is God incarnate, not to carry forth Jesus' liberating work. There is little, according to this interpretation, to compel a Christian to participate in social justice movements. Protest activity is incidental to what it means to be a good Christian. Such disregard for protest implicates the White Christ in Black oppression.

Black identity is inextricably linked to protests resulting from being non-White in a society defined by White racism. To suggest that protest activity is irrelevant to Christ is to suggest that Blackness is irrelevant to Christ. Further, the passivity in relation to social injustice, which the White Christ fosters, allows White racism to go unchallenged. In essence the White Christ, as it was carried forth by southern White clergy, negated a significant aspect of Black identity while it permitted White Christians to ignore Black people's claims for freedom.

The Reality of the Black Christ

Martin King questioned which God southern White clergy were following: "Who is their God? Is their God the God of Abraham, Isaac and Jacob? And is their Savior the Savior who hung on the cross at Golgotha?"[3] He did not understand how a person could claim to follow the Christian gospel and at the same time tacitly support racism. He strongly opposed a view of Christianity and Jesus that could lead to quietism in the face of injustice.

King's interpretation of Jesus Christ formed the foundation for his participation in the 1960s Black freedom movement. Reminiscent of the slave Christianity of his ancestors, a tradition that he undoubtedly encountered through growing up in the Black church, this foundation reflected the religion of the Black Christ. It did so in at least three areas: (1) the relationship between Black people and God; (2) the meaning of freedom; and (3) the compatibility between Christianity and protest activity.

The Relationship between Black People and God

Sometimes King spoke about God without referring directly to Jesus. What he said about God, however, was rarely divorced from his understanding of Jesus. The God he spoke of was the Christian God. His interpretation of God's significance was inextricably related to his interpretation of Jesus' significance.

King's understanding of the relationship between Black people and God began with his recognition that they were God's children. He frequently referred to Black people as "children of God."[4] Although he did not consider Black people God's *only* children, the fact that he included them as a part of God's human family was significant. This claim refuted any White racist assumptions that Black people were something less than human, and therefore not due any respect as human beings.

King defined what it meant for Black people to be "children of God" in terms of God's active presence in their lives. He believed that God identified with them in their struggle to be free, and that God sustained them during that struggle. His "kitchen table experience" clearly reveals his confidence in God's identification with Black people.[5]

Late one January night, in the midst of the Montgomery, Alabama, bus boycott, a phone caller said to King: "Listen, nigger, we've taken all we want from you; before next week you'll be sorry you ever came to Montgomery." This call was one of many threats that King received during his involvement in the civil rights movement. But this particular threat deeply disturbed him. Unable to sleep, he got out of bed to make a cup of coffee:

> With my cup of coffee sitting untouched before me I tried to think of a way to move out of the picture without appearing a coward. . . . I decided to take my problem to God. With my head in my hands, I bowed over the kitchen table and prayed aloud. . . . "I am here taking a stand for what I believe is right. But now I am afraid. The people are looking to me for leadership, and if I stand before them without strength and courage, they too will falter. I am at the end of my powers. I have nothing left. I've come to the point where I can't face it alone."[6]

At that moment King says he "experienced the presence of the Divine" as he had never experienced it before. He heard an inner voice answering his prayer: "Stand up for righteousness, stand up for truth; and God will be at your side forever."[7] James Cone explains that after this experience, King "never doubted God's presence in the struggle for justice."[8]

This same experience reassured King not only that God was with him and other Black protestors in their battle against White racism, but that God sustained Black people. When he grew tired and frustrated, he often recounted his "kitchen table experience" as an inspiration to continue the civil rights struggle. David Garrow says this existential experience with God gave King "new strength and courage."[9] King reminded Black people of God's sustaining presence during some of their most difficult times. At the funeral for three of the four little Black girls killed in the bombing of a Birmingham, Alabama, church, he told the mourning congregation that God would lift them "from fatigue of despair to the buoyancy of hope, and transform dark and desolate valleys into sunlit paths of inner peace."[10]

What allowed King to be so sure that the voice he heard at his kitchen table was God's, and not merely a projection of his own inner voice? Why was he certain that God identified with Black people in their struggle for freedom? How did he know that God sustained Black people during their difficult times? The answers to these questions reflect an interpretation of Christianity that forms the foundation for the Black Christ.

For King, God's significance was determined by God's *liberating actions* within history. Pointing to God's active involvement, he sometimes referred to God as "the God of history."[11] In one sermon he observed:

Above all, we must be reminded anew that God is at work in his universe. He is not outside the world looking on with a sort of cold indifference. Here on all the roads of life he is striving in our striving. Like an everloving Father he is working through history for the salvation of *his children.*[12]

The Israelites' exodus from Egypt was one event that King often used as evidence of God's liberating activity in history. He described how God prevented the Egyptian army from crossing the Red Sea, and thus helped to free the Israelites from slavery.[13] Like the Black slaves before him, he believed that God identified with Black people as God had identified with the Israelites. What God did for the Israelites in Egypt, God would do for the Black oppressed in the United States. Frequently comparing the Black situation to the Israelite situation, King was confident that "the God of history" would help free Black people from the evil of White racism the way God helped free the Israelites from Egyptian bondage.

In addition to suggesting God's identification with the Black oppressed, the exodus event also suggested to King that God would sustain Black people in their struggle to be free. He preached:

> We must also remember that God does not forget *his children* who are the victims of evil forces. He gives us the interior resources to bear the burdens and tribulations of life. When we are in the darkness of some oppressive Egypt God is a light unto our path. He imbues us with the strength needed to endure the ordeals of Egypt, and he gives us the courage and power to undertake the journey ahead. When the lamp of hope flickers and the candle of faith runs low, he restoreth our souls, giving us renewed vigour to carry on.[14]

By accenting the fact that Black people were "children of God," King made clear that they were entitled to the same rights as other human beings, and more importantly, that God cared about them just as God cared about all people. By underscoring that God identified with and sustained Black people in their struggle to be free, King also defied any arguments that might suggest that God favored or was passive in relation to Black oppression.

The Meaning of Freedom

King's interpretation of Christian freedom also remains consistent with the slave religion tradition and thus reflects the religion of the Black Christ. Similiar to his slave ancestors, he did not completely spiritualize the Christian concept of freedom. While the freedom that Jesus offered may have had "heavenly implications," King did not consider it limited to heaven. He believed Jesus' freedom could be experienced in history. His understanding of Christian freedom as an earthly possibility is revealed not just by his protest activity, but also in his public addresses and in the freedom songs that characterized the movement.

In his speeches, as well as in his sermons, King often connected Black people's quest for historical freedom directly to God or Jesus. He frequently did this by concluding discussions about freedom with the spirituals, which expressed the slaves' desire for freedom. In one speech he punctuated his observations concerning the urgency to be free with the slave spiritual, "Oh, Freedom! Oh, Freedom."[15] He brought his much quoted "I Have a Dream" speech to an emotional peak with the following declaration:

> And when we allow freedom to ring . . . we will be able to speed up the day when all of God's children . . . will be able to join hands and to sing in the words of the Old Negro spiritual "Free at last free at last; thank God Almighty, we are free at last.[16]

By consistently maintaining the link between Christian freedom and Black people's contemporary struggle for freedom, King clarified his belief that the freedom that God offers through Jesus is not merely a "heavenly" possibility—it is also a historical possibility.

The "freedom songs," which King called "the soul" of the civil rights movement, also clearly demonstrate his understanding of Christian freedom. Although slave spirituals were the source for many of these freedom songs, civil rights protestors revised them to fit their own contemporary situation. If the meaning of Christian freedom was sometimes ambiguous in the spirituals when the slaves sang them, it was not by the time Black protestors reshaped and sung them. For instance, Black protestors added the verses "no more segregation" and "no more Jim Crow" to the slave spiritual "Oh, Freedom! Oh, Freedom." They transformed the slaves' refrain, "I want Jesus to walk with me/ All along this pilgrim journey," to "I want Jesus to walk with me/All along this Freedom Journey."[17] King affirmed the civil rights protestors' contemporary interpretations of the slave spirituals. He said, "For the same reasons the slaves sang, Negroes today sing freedom songs. For we, too, are in bondage. We sing out of our determination that 'We shall overcome.' "[18]

Why was King so confident that the freedom offered by Jesus could be attained on earth? Like the creators of slave Christianity, King interpreted the freedom that Jesus offered in light of Old Testament stories concerning God's freedom. The prophetic narratives greatly influenced him. These narratives stressed God's intention for freedom to become a historical reality in the Israelite kingdom. King was especially drawn to the prophet Amos. Whereas the slaves often compared Jesus to Moses, he often compared Jesus to Amos.[19] He equated Jesus' freedom with Amos's call for "justice to run down like waters and righteousness like an ever-flowing stream."[20] Amos's prophetic narrative provided King with a foundation to define Jesus' freedom as something attainable on earth. Like its impact on the slaves, Christ's freedom did not render King passive, but inspired him to rebel against racial injustice.

The Compatibility between Christianity and Protest Activity

If God identifies with Black people and sustains them in their struggle for freedom, and if Jesus offers a freedom that is attainable in history, then it is appropriate—if not required—for Christians to rebel against any social barrier to Black people's freedom. King believed that there was a compatibility between Christianity and protest activity.

In his first public speech during the Montgomery bus boycott —commonly referred to as the Holt Street Address—he clearly articulated the affinity between being a Christian and being a protestor against racial injustice. Throughout this address, King accented the fact that the boycotters were Christian. He also made a direct link between the teachings of Jesus and the Montgomery protest:

> I want it to be known that we are a Christian people. We believe in the Christian religion. We believe in the teachings of Jesus. The only weapon we have in our hand this evening is the weapon of protest.[21]

Continuing to stress the compatibility between Christianity and the boycott, he strongly proclaimed:

we are not wrong in what we are doing. . . . If we are wrong
God Almighty is wrong. If we are wrong Jesus of Nazareth
was merely a utopian dreamer and never came down to
earth. If we are wrong justice is a lie. And we are determined. . . . to work and fight until "justice runs down like
water and righteousness like a mighty stream."[22]

King's first public address as the leader of the civil rights
movement parallels the Lukan version of Jesus' first public
address:

> The spirit of the Lord is upon me
> because he has anointed me;
> he has sent me to announce good news to the poor,
> to proclaim release for prisoners and recovery of
>   sight for the blind;
> to let the broken victims go free,
> to proclaim the year of the Lord's
> favour (Luke 4:18–19).

Both King's and Jesus' speeches are characterized by a call
to protest social injustice. Jesus linked protest activity to what
it meant for him to be Christ. King linked protest activity to
what it meant for him to be a Christian. King's Holt Street
address compares with Jesus' sermon at Nazareth as a concise
example of the religion of the Black Christ.

On many other occasions, King referred to Jesus' Nazareth
sermon. For him, Jesus' words, "The Spirit of the Lord is upon
me because he has anointed me to preach good news to the
poor," were central to understanding the demands of the Christian gospel. He said these words illustrated that "Christianity is
itself a protest."[23] This belief was apparently what made King
certain that the boycotters "were not wrong in what they were
doing." They were merely heeding Jesus' challenge to protest
social injustice.

King's claim that all Christians are challenged, if not obli-
gated, to protest racial injustice has strong implications for salvation. King suggested that salvation involves more than
confessing Jesus as Lord. It involves doing what Jesus com-

manded. King, obviously thinking of Matthew 25:31f., put it sharply:

> One day we will stand before the God of history. . . .
> It seems that I can hear the God of history saying . . . I was hungry and ye fed me not. I was naked and ye clothed me not. I was devoid of a decent sanitary house to live in, and ye provided no shelter for me. And consequently, you cannot enter the kingdom of greatness. If ye do it unto the least of these my brethen, ye do it unto me.[24]

For King there was no incompatibility between Christianity and protest activity. He believed that the two were inextricably connected. Jesus' liberating ministry, especially his teachings, challenged all Christians to protest any form of social oppression. To be a Christian means that one has no choice but to protest injustice, in this particular instance racial injustice.

Like the slave religion before him, King's words and actions demonstrated how Christianity can become a critique of a White racist status quo. Interpreters of King have suggested that he restored the proper relationship between Christianity and social justice. He in fact carried the religion of the Black Christ into twentieth-century America. He prevented Christianity from being seen only as a "sacred canopy" for White dominance. He made it clear that Christ stood against White racism and that Christ compelled Christians to do the same.

But just as slave religion did not make the color of Christ an issue during the antebellum period, King did not do so during the 1960s Black freedom movement. Again, Black nationalists would be the ones to articulate the need for a physically Black Christ. No contemporary nationalist raised the issue of Christ's color more forcefully than the Black Muslim, Malcolm X. Malcolm X's Black nationalist philosophy was a catalyst for a movement in the Black community that made it impossible for the Black church and Black theologians to remain silent concerning the color of Christ.

MALCOLM X AND THE COLOR OF CHRIST

While King and many White clergy were in disagreement over the proper way to interpret the Christian gospel, especially as it related to the Black struggle, Malcolm X was vociferously pro-claiming that Christianity itself was detrimental to Black free-dom. He argued that it was a religious tool used by the slaveholders to keep Black people "happy go lucky" on earth with their "eyes fixed on pie in the sky and heaven in the here-after."[25] Emphasizing Christianity's turn-the-other-cheek ethic was one means slaveholders used, according to Malcolm X, to keep their slaves passive and content on earth.[26] For Malcolm X, King's movement—particularly because of its nonviolent strategy and emphasis on love of the enemy (more will be said about this later)—was merely an example of the "slaveholder's religion" in practice.

On the one hand, Malcolm X's critique of Christianity as an oppressive religion did not reveal an awareness of the distinction between slaveholding Christianity and slave Christianity. While some slaves did accept slaveholding Christianity's "other-worldly" emphasis, many others did not accept it. Perhaps Mal-colm X's failure to recognize this distinction prevented him from perceiving the difference between King's understanding of Jesus and many southern White churchgoers' understanding of Jesus. Regardless of the particular nonviolent tactics that King adopted, his understanding supported Black people in their fight to be free, while the dominant southern White church under-standing of Jesus did not.

On the other hand, Malcolm X's apparent failure to appre-ciate the various interpretations of the Christian gospel did not invalidate his most penetrating critique of Christianity. This cri-tique focused on the color of Jesus Christ. King's understanding of Christ, like slave Christianity before him, did not seem to appreciate the significance of what Christ looked like, or was portrayed to look like. But Malcolm X's concerns about Christ did. He realized the blasphemy involved in Black people's wor-shiping a Christ who looked just like the White people who oppressed and terrorized them. Malcolm X poignantly observed that while religions of other people made them proud of who they were, Christianity "was designed to make [black people] feel inferior."[27] It achieved its purpose, he said, by giving Black people a "blond, blue-eyed, pale-skinned 'god'. . . to worship and admire."[28]

Was Malcolm revealing an inherent weakness in Christianity? Even if one could claim that a White Christ represents a distortion of the Christian religion, did the mere possibility for distortion indicate a problem? If Christianity can produce a White Christ, and in fact has a long history of doing so, is there not something inherently wrong with Christianity and its Jesus?[29] Whatever the answer to this question, Malcolm X was clear that Black peoples' loyalty to a White Christ was a betrayal of their own Black heritage, Black culture, and was a severe impediment to their freedom.

Malcolm's scathing criticisms of the White Christ could not go ignored. Black psychologist Kenneth Clark had already explained, in his arguments before the United States Supreme Court during the 1954 *Brown versus the Board of Education* case, how important it was for Black people, particularly Black children, to have positive Black images. His research demonstrated that a bombardment of White images and symbols severely damages Black self-worth and self-esteem.[30] Essentially, Clark's findings supported Malcolm X's observation that Black worship of White images—even Christ—is unhealthy, and reflective of Black people's psychological and emotional enslavement to a White racist culture.

That Malcolm X's stringent attacks on Christianity and its White Christ were not ignored, is reflected in the concern voiced by the media over these claims. In the 1959 television series on the Black Muslims, "The Hate that Hate Produced," reporters Louis Lomax and Mike Wallace raised the issue of the color of Jesus. Disturbed by Black nationalists' "call on Negroes to reject the white man's conception of Jesus as white," Lomax questioned Black churchwoman Anna Arnold Hedgeman about the importance of Jesus' color, and about her own remarks that apparently affirmed Jesus' Blackness. In response to Lomax, Hedgeman declared that while Jesus may not have been Black "he certainly was not white."[31] She then went on to suggest that it was important for Black people to be able to see Jesus as one of them, as Black-skinned, since they lived in a country where the color of one's skin was a significant factor.

While it was Martin who kept alive the slave religion tradition by insisting that Christ was a liberator of Black people, it was

Malcolm who kept alive the nationalist tradition by pointing to the necessity of Christ being Black. Malcolm recognized the link between having positive Black images and Black self-esteem. In order for Christ to have any meaning for Black people as they struggled for their freedom from White racism, Christ would have to be a combination of Martin and Malcolm: a liberator who was actually Black. If Martin and Malcolm did not make this clear, the demands from the young Black Power advocates, sometimes referred to as "the angry children of Malcolm X," certainly made it clear.[32]

The Angry Children of Malcolm X Call for a Black Christ

Prior to advocating Black Power, the young Black protestors of the Student Non-Violent Coordinating Committee (SNCC) supported King's commitment to love, nonviolence, and an integrated society. The founding statement of SNCC opened:

We affirm the philosophical or religious ideal of non-violence as the foundation of our purpose, the presupposition of our faith and the manner of our action. Non-violence as it grows from Judaic-Christian tradition seeks a social order of justice permeated by love. Integration of human endeavor represents the first steps toward such a society.[33]

As a result of their commitment to King's protest strategy, SNCC members conducted nonviolent campaigns throughout the South, which were aimed toward integrating Black people into the wider society. Eventually, however, SNCC's Black protestors grew impatient with King's nonviolent strategy. Not being allowed to defend themselves against White people's brutal attacks, they were frustrated. They were fed up with risking their lives for what appeared to be minimal changes in the White racist social-political structure. They were ready to abandon King's Christian concepts of love, nonviolence, and integration.

As pointed out above, King's commitment to justice was reminiscent of slave Christianity and thus the religion of the Black Christ. His strategy of love and nonviolence, however, was not necessarily reflective of slave Christianity and was not an inevitable outgrowth of the Black Christ. His protest strategy was determined by his interpretation of Jesus' cross.

King interpreted Jesus' cross as a symbol of love, redemptive suffering, and commitment to God's kingdom. He argued that because of a deep love for all humanity, Jesus willingly suffered on the cross so that humanity might experience the kingdom of God. This understanding of the cross was the basis for King's adoption of a nonviolent protest strategy.[34] He believed that Black people were called to bear Jesus' cross for humanity. This meant that as Jesus willingly suffered for the sake of God's kingdom, Black people were called to willingly suffer for the sake of the "beloved community."[35] They would have to experience a "season of suffering" in order to achieve a just society.[36] This emphasis on love, redemptive suffering, and the beloved community translated into nonviolent resistance to racist social policies, "turning the other cheek" to White violent responses, and a commitment to achieving an integrated society.

Although, especially at the beginning of his civil rights involvement, King did not separate a commitment to Jesus' love from a commitment to Jesus' justice, in practice, love seemed to overshadow justice. For example, young Black protestors committed themselves to using King's nonviolent strategy, but justice was not the immediate result of this strategy. The immediate and most visible reward was White hostility. King's protest strategy seemed to obscure the radicality of his understanding of Jesus.

On the one hand, young Black protestors' break with King was not reflective of their doubt in King's commitment to justice. Rather, their break reflected a disillusionment with King's understanding of Christian love. Vincent Harding observed that young Black protestors broke with King because he "was trying to get [them] to love white folks before [they] learned to love [themselves]."[37] The Black protestors expressed their sentiments in song:

> Too much love,
> Too much love,
> Nothing kills a nigger,
> Like too much love.[38]

On the other hand, young Black protestors' break with King did imply that an emphasis on Jesus' commitment to justice was not enough. It did not necessarily mean that Jesus supported Black self-love. The urgency for a Black Christ was beginning to crystalize. In their turning away from King, the Black Power advocates revealed a need for an understanding of Jesus Christ that not only compelled Black people to fight for their freedom, but also invested them with pride in their own Black selves. If King and his "Christian" principles were not going to liberate Black people from the physical *and* psychological bonds of White racism, then Black Power advocates were more than willing to leave both King and Christianity behind. The young Black students of SNCC in fact did this when they turned toward Malcolm X.

Although Malcolm X had been assassinated by the time they broke with King, having encountered Malcolm's thought as they moved from the rural South to the urban centers of the North, he provided the young Black protestors with a foundation for their Black Power movement. In turning toward his nationalist philosophy, they encountered a strategy of protest that was diametrically opposed to King's. Whereas King's philosophy was characterized by love for all humanity, redemptive suffering, and an integrated society, Malcolm X's was characterized by self-love, self-defense, and Black independence. For King, nonviolent protest was the only appropiate way that Black people could achieve a just society. For Malcolm X, Black people could use "any means necessary" to achieve justice.

Not only was Malcolm's protest strategy appealing to the young Black protestors, but so too were his stringent criticisms of Christianity. He seemed to have voiced what these protestors were feeling when they decided to break with King. Again, their break implied that they needed a religion that supported them in their Blackness. Their turn toward Malcolm X signified that they agreed with him: Christianity, with its White Christ, was not that religion.

This turn toward Malcolm X eventually gave way to the Black consciousness era with its shouts of Black Power. Could Christianity and its Jesus support this new Black attitude? Was there room in Christianity for a Christ who wore the face of both Martin and Malcolm?

Black Clergy Speak

One of the earliest public theological responses to this question came from a group of radical Black clergy. Feeling pressed by the mood and sentiments of the Black community, they met to discuss the implications of Black Power for Christianity. As one Black religious leader explained, "There was the feeling that we needed to speak . . . that Black Power was nothing new theologically and that [Black Power] was within the purview of the Christian church."[39] With the cry for Black Power being criticized from leaders in both the Black and White communities, including by Martin King, these clergy sought to discern the compatibility between the gospel of Jesus Christ and Black power.

Coming together as the National Committee of Negro Churchmen (NCNC, later to become the National Conference of Black Chuchmen, NCBC), Black clergy leaders issued a statement in the July 31, 1966, edition of the *New York Times* that endorsed Black Power. This statement opened by describing the contemporary American scene as one where "conscienceless power meets powerless conscience."[40] It said that White people had power but no moral conscience, and Black people had moral conscience but no power. The consequence of this imbalance was that conscienceless White people have "aped" God, thereby usurping privileges of power over others, which only God is to have; while powerless Black people have developed a form of love that "becomes chaotic self-surrender." The solution was for all persons, Black as well as Whites, to have both power and conscience. The Black clergy statement concluded that "from the point of view of the Christian faith, there is nothing necessarily wrong with concern for power."[41]

This *New York Times* statement laid the foundation for an even more explicit articulation of what Jesus Christ had to do with Black Power and the Black quest for freedom. In June, 1969, NCBC issued a statement that proclaimed:

The message of liberation is the revelation of God as revealed in the incarnation of Jesus Christ. Freedom **IS** the gospel. Jesus is the Liberator! . . . Thus the black patriarchs and we ourselves know this reality despite all attempts of the white church to obscure it and to utilize Christianity as a means of enslaving blacks. The demand that Christ the Liberator imposes on all men *requires* all blacks to affirm their full dignity as persons and all whites to surrender their presumptions of superiority and abuses of power.[42]

This 1969 statement attempted to portray Jesus Christ as a combination of Martin and Malcolm. It explicitly affirmed Martin and the slave religion tradition by declaring Christ as a liberator of Black people. It was less explicit, however, concerning the reality of Christ's Blackness. It stated that Christ affirmed Black humanity, but it did not clarify whether or not Christ was actually Black.

While the clergy of NCBC made great strides in showing the relevancy of the Christian gospel for a "proud" Black people, there was still work to be done. Black theologians would bring to fruition the seeds planted by Martin and Malcolm, and watered by NCBC, in the quest for a Black Christ.

Chapter 3

THE THEOLOGICAL DEVELOPMENT OF THE BLACK CHRIST

By the end of the 1960s, Black consciousness had erupted within northern cities. Black people living in urban ghettoes rebelled against all that denied their humanity. They burned, looted, and destroyed the signs of their oppression. They set their neighborhoods on fire and put their lives on the line for their dignity and freedom. The refrain, "Say it Loud, I'm Black and I'm Proud," gave way to "Burn baby Burn." Did Jesus Christ have any meaning for a people "on fire" with self-respect and a vision for freedom? Now was the time for theologians to speak.

With a few exceptions White theologians followed the pattern that Southern White clergy maintained—they remained silent on issues of racial injustice. They carried forth the religion of the White Christ. They did not address Christ's significance in relation to the Black struggle against White racism. Their failure to relate the gospel message to the inhumane treatment of Black people in a White racist society suggested that Christ was unconcerned with Black oppression.

White theologians were also unwilling to acknowledge that the Black experience had anything to contribute toward understanding Christ's meaning for contemporary society. As Joseph Johnson, Jr., explained, White theologians never conceived of Jesus "walking the dark streets of the ghettoes of the North and the sharecropper's farm in the Deep South."[1] Essentially, consistent with the religion of the White Christ, White theologians

53

saw no connection between Blackness and the gospel of Jesus. A group of Black theologians saw something different. They believed that the Christian gospel and Blackness were inextricably related. Albert Cleage, James Cone, and J. Deotis Roberts, each in his own way, pronounced that Christ was Black. As different as their three versions are, when presented today they each get very different responses.

Cleage, while a pastor of a Detroit church and a close associate of Malcolm X, declared that Christ was literally Black. When I have lectured to Black church groups, especially young adults or teenagers, or to Black seminarians, this version of the Black Christ causes the most discussion and excitement. After hearing about Cleage's interpretation of Christ's Blackness, they typically ask where they can get more information on Jesus' ancestry and possible African connections. This is perhaps reflective of the emergence of the Afrocentric movement in the Black community where particularly academics and young Black people are concerned to discover the richness of Black people's African heritage.

When presenting Cone's version in the same or similiar contexts, it has often received much criticism and resistance. Cone, while a professor at a small college outside Detroit who was angered by White theologians' failure to address the Black condition, proclaimed that in twentieth-century America Christ must be Black. For a Black church people in a post–civil rights era who enjoy the "privileges" of an integrated society, or who at least dream for this type of society, anything that appears to potentially divide them against White people is unacceptable. Consequently, in contexts in which I have been a part, Black churchgoers and seminarians have often protested that Cone's version of the Black Christ is too exclusive and confrontational.

It is often Roberts's version that receives the most overall acceptance by Black churchgoers and seminarians. Roberts, while a professor at Howard University who was guided by a vision of Black and White together, acknowledged that it was important to see Christ as Black. This version, which emphasizes reconciliation, seems to have much appeal to a people striving for a society of "Black and White together."

This chapter will seek to discern whether perceptions of

Cleage's, Cone's, and Roberts's version of the Black Christ are accurate. In so doing, the distinctiveness of each version will be explored in discussions concerning the relationship between Blackness and Christ, the significance of liberation and reconciliation, and the appropriateness of violence or nonviolence for the Black freedom struggle.

THE RELATIONSHIP BETWEEN BLACKNESS AND CHRIST

Cleage's Version

Albert Cleage put forth the most provocative version of Christ's Blackness. He argued that Jesus of Nazareth was ethnically Black. He explained:

When I say Jesus was black, that Jesus was the black Messiah, I'm not saying "Wouldn't it be nice if Jesus was black?" or "Let's pretend that Jesus was black," or "It's necessary psychologically for us to believe that Jesus was black." I'm saying that Jesus WAS black.[2]

Cleage based his vehement claims about Jesus' Blackness on Jesus' bloodline—which he traced through Jesus' mother, Mary. Mary, Cleage pointed out, was a member of the Israelite tribe of Judah, which consisted of a "non-white black people in the same sense that Arabs were black people, in the same sense that Egyptians were black people."[3] Cleage supported his claims that the tribe of Judah was "non-white" by explaining that the Israelites were a "mixture of Chaldeans, Egyptians, Midianites, Ethiopians, Kushites, Babylonians and other dark peoples, all of whom were already mixed with black people of Central Africa."[4] Cleage concluded: "Jesus was a Black Messiah born to a Black woman."[5]

When Cleage called Jesus Black, he was referring to more than Jesus' dark-skinned complexion. As his genealogical emphasis suggested, and as shall be seen more clearly later in this chapter, he was saying that Jesus was ethnically Black in the same sense that Black Americans were Black. He used the genealogical data to suggest that Jesus was of African ancestry and had an ancestral relationship to Black Americans.

Even though his understanding of Jesus' Blackness was primarily predicated upon Jesus' human parentage, Cleage did not ignore Jesus' divine parentage. While he did not entertain a concept of God becoming incarnate in Jesus, he did stress the fact that Jesus was God's son. This fact further supported his conclusion that Jesus was Black. It did this as Cleage established God's Blackness. He argued:

> But if God created man in his own image, then we must look at man to see what God looks like. There are black men, there are yellow men, there are red men and there are a few, a mighty few, white men in the world. If God created man in his own image, then God must be some combination of this black, red, yellow and white . . . we must think of God as a Black God. . . . In America, one drop of black blood makes you black. So by American law, God is black.[6]

Cleage's version of Christ's Blackness was essentially based on the fact that Jesus was the Black son of a Black Israelite woman and of a Black God. Jesus' Blackness was primarily grounded on historical, genealogical data, and secondarily on God's likeness to humanity.

Why was Cleage so adamant about Jesus' actual ethnicity? Why was it important for him that "the Messiah" be literally Black? At least three factors suggest answers to these questions: his role as pastor, his understanding of the Black church, and his ties to Black nationalism.

Cleage, as indicated earlier, was the pastor of a Black church in the heart of Detroit's Black ghetto. He pastored this church during the height of Detroit's racial rebellions. Like many other Black pastors of that time, Cleage was concerned with what he was going to say to his parishioners on Sunday mornings in light of the ongoing Black struggle. He needed to find a way to make the Christian gospel relevant to a Black people who rarely experienced relief from the psychological and physical burdens of White racism. One way in which to do this was to establish that Jesus Christ was thoroughly committed to Black people. To say that Jesus was literally Black seemed to accomplish this.

Cleage's "quest for a Black Messiah" was also motivated by what he perceived to be the Black church's captivity to slave-holding Christianity. For the most part, he saw the Black church as a barrier to Black freedom. He said it harbored a slaveholding religion that kept Black people focused on "heaven" for comfort. He described the Black church as "a survival instrument," which "helped maintain sanity, but . . . destroyed the possibility for a united black liberation struggle."[7]

In addition, Cleage shared the contention of his close friend and associate Malcolm X that the worship of a White Christ was the most enslaving feature of the Black church. He argued that if Black people continued to worship a blond-haired, blue-eyed Jesus, then they would never be free from the shackles of White racism:

Black people cannot build dignity on their knees worship-ping a white Christ. We must put down this white Jesus which the white man gave us in slavery and which has been tearing us to pieces.[8]

In an effort to move the Black community toward freedom from White racism, Cleage felt compelled to rescue the Black church from its enslavement to slaveholding Christianity. An important step in this liberating process was to free Black people from the worship of a White Jesus.

As important as the needs of his Black parishioners and his perceived ineffectiveness of the Black church were in motivating his "quest for a Black Messiah," the most influential factor was his Black nationalist ties. Cleage was often in dialogue with Black nationalists such as Malcolm X, Stokely Carmichael, as well as Richard and Milton Henry, both of whom were at one time members of Cleage's church. Cleage's own vision for a Black nation was reflective of Black nationalism's goals for a liberated Black community.[9] Yet Cleage, though a nationalist in thought, was not willing to give up his Christian heritage. He recognized that as insightful as nationalists may have been concerning the Black problem, they were rarely able to capture the majority of the Black population—a primarily Christian popu-

lation.[10] Cleage believed that there was a need to bring together — in much the same way that Marcus Garvey had done —
Black nationalism with Christianity. If he could show that Christianity was in fact not White but Black in its origin, and that it
was centered around a Black Messiah, then he had a way of
adopting a Black nationalist perspective while not disregarding
Black peoples' Christian heritage.

Essentially, it was Cleage's identity as a Black nationalist that
compelled him to conduct a quest for an ethnically Black Jesus.
A non-Black Jesus would have forced him to make a choice
between nationalism and Christianity, his Blackness, and his
religion. By proclaiming that Jesus was a Black man Cleage
avoided that choice and provided other Black Christians with a
way to do the same.

Cone's Version

James Cone offered a symbolic version of Christ's Blackness.
In this version Blackness did not refer to Jesus' ethnic characteristics. It was a symbol of Jesus' existential commitments. In
this regard, Blackness was not incidental to who Christ was, but
was an essential aspect of Christ's nature.

In developing his argument for Christ's Blackness, Cone bor-
rowed from Paul Tillich's definition of ontological symbols. Tillich recognized that humans, finite beings, could not adequately
express or capture in words the divine, an infinite being. Ontological symbols, he said, were the only means that humans had
available to them for communicating about the divine. These
symbols have at least four characteristics: they point beyond
themselves to the divine, they participate in that to which they
point, they "unlock" aspects of the divine reality that otherwise
might be closed to humans, and they open up "hidden depths"
of human reality.[11]

Cone argued that to affirm Christ as Black was the best way
to represent Christ's contemporary presence in Black people's
lives. As an ontological symbol Black pointed to the essence of
the Black experience in "twentieth-century America" and to the
contemporary identity of Jesus as Christ. Cone defined the Black
experience as a constant struggle to survive and become free

from White racism. He argued that discrimination against Black people was primarily connected to the color of their skin. "Since the black community is an oppressed community because and only because of its blackness," Cone proclaimed, "the Christological importance of Jesus Christ must be found in his blackness."[12]

Black people's oppression was not the only decisive factor in Cone's calling Christ "Black"; there was also the fact that Jesus identified with the oppressed during his own time. Reflective of slave Christianity, Cone argued that Jesus' commitment to the oppressed characterized what it meant for him to be Christ. He stressed the importance of Jesus' identifying with the oppressed in his birth, ministry, and death.

For Cone then, Christ's Blackness was informed by Jesus' historical identification with the oppressed, and by the fact that in a White racist society, Black people were the oppressed ones. Cone explained: "Christ is black, therefore, not because of some cultural or psychological need of black people, but because and only because God *really* enters into the world where the poor, the despised and the oppressed are."[13]

Some interpreters of Cone have had difficulty comprehending what Cone means when he calls Christ Black. They have critiqued him as if he uses the term literally. They claim that his theology is too exclusive of White people.[14]

Cone does sometimes use the term "Black" literally, but not in the sense that Cleage uses it literally. The "vagueness" of the use of "Black" in Cone's theology is typical of ontological symbols. If an ontological symbol points to human as well as divine reality, then as much as it corresponds to a particular human condition, it has a literal aspect. With Cone's version of the Black Christ, Black is literal in relationship to human reality, but symbolic in relationship to the divine. He explained:

> Theological language must be paradoxical because of the necessity of affirming two dimensions of reality which appear to be contradictory. . . . Through my particular experience of blackness, I encounter the symbolic significance of black existence and how that existence is related to God's revelation in Jesus Christ.[15]

Though a proper understanding of Cone's Black Christ dictates an appreciation for the symbolic meaning of Black, a recognition of the literal aspect of Christ's Blackness is also crucial. It was essential that Christ be inextricably linked to the particularity of Black oppression. This link had special significance to Cone.

While Cleage was serving as pastor in the Detroit ghetto, Cone was teaching at a White college (Adrian College) about seventy miles outside Detroit. Already questioning the relevance of Christian theology to Black people's suffering, the question became even more urgent for Cone after the 1967 Detroit riot.[16] He felt that he could no longer remain silent about God's relationship to Black people while, in Detroit, forty-three people were killed in the struggle for Black dignity and freedom, and others were being killed all over America. He was also "outraged" not just at White theologians' silence concerning racial injustice, but at those White theologians and ministers who condemned Black violence while saying nothing about the daily systemic violence perpetrated against Black people. Cone needed to find a means to relate the Christian gospel to the Black experience in a way that did not condemn Black people's responses to their oppression. He also wanted a way to force White theologians to deal with Black people's particular reality. To say that Christ was literally Black in twentieth-century America accomplished Cone's objectives. Cone's own explanation makes clear the fundamental significance of Christ's literal Blackness:

> First, blackness is a *physiological* trait. It refers to a particular black-skinned people in America, a victim of white racist brutality. The scars of its members bear witness to the inhumanity committed against them. Black theology believes that they are the *only* key that can open the door to divine revelation. Therefore, no American theology can even tend in the direction of Christian theology without coming to terms with the black-skinned people of America.[17]

Roberts's Version

Like Cone, J. Deotis Roberts provided a more symbolic understanding of what it meant for Christ to be Black. But while

Cone used Black to point to Christ's particular relationship with the oppressed, Roberts used it to emphasize Christ's universal relationship to all of humanity.

Roberts's version of the Black Christ began with an understanding of the incarnation. Roberts argued that in becoming incarnate, becoming Christ, God identified with all humanity. Christ's significance was found, not in Christ's special relation with a particular group of people, but in Christ's universal relationship with all people.

Yet, while Roberts stressed the significance of Christ's universal identification with humanity, he did not overlook the particular aspect of Christ's identification with humanity. He understood Christ's particular interest, however, in relationship to Christ's universal interest. Roberts argued that because Christ identified with all people, Christ identified with each person in his or her own historical particularity. He put it this way: "The gospel is both universal and particular. Jesus is the Savior of each and the Lord of all."[18] This understanding of the universal Christ, who identified with humans in their particularities, formed the basis for Roberts's interpretation of what Black meant in relation to Christ.

Roberts argued that if the universal Christ came to all people in their particular historical context, then all people had a right to define Christ through their particular experience and image Christ in their own likeness. Black people had as much right to see Christ in their own likeness as did White, Red, Yellow, and Brown people.

Roberts was further prompted to call Christ Black because he recognized the importance of Black people's being able to image Christ as Black. He said:

> The most difficult task for the Black man is to obtain psychological freedom. If he can accept his Blackness, be proud of it and find meaning for his life, he can know true inner freedom. This is where Jesus, as the Black Messiah, comes in. The Black Messiah enables the Black man to stand up to life. . . .
>
> It is not difficult to understand why a Black Christ who

comes to the Black man in his blackness and identifies with his lot can bring succor and comfort to the Black man.[19]

As with Cleage and Cone, Roberts was motivated to call Christ Black because of the nature of Black people's oppression. Also like Cleage and Cone, Roberts's Black Christ was not strictly based on the need for Black people to see Christ as Black. Roberts suggested that Christ's Blackness was an aspect of what it meant for God to become incarnate. He concluded that like the White Christ, or Red Christ, "the Black Messiah is also the universal word made flesh."[20]

Why did Roberts feel compelled to emphasize Christ's universality? Why was he concerned to show that Christ was not just Black but for all people? Why, at a time when the dominant theological tradition ignored the Black particularity, did Roberts emphasize Christ's universal relationship to all humanity as opposed to Christ's particular relationship to Black people?

Some speculated that the reason for Roberts's emphasis on Christ's universalism was because he did not want to become alienated from the White "theological roundtable."[21] This explanation perhaps had merit and was perhaps at the root of Roberts's focus on Christ's universalism, but Roberts later revealed another genuine concern. He explained that he came to Black theology from an interest and study of world religions. He was acutely aware of the diversity of religions, as well as the diversity within Christianity. His stress on universality was a way of allowing Christ to have meaning for people in diverse contexts.[22] Basically, Roberts wanted to develop an image of Christ that was not potentially exclusive or oppressive of others. He wanted to make sure that Black theologians did not make "Jesus a captive of black culture as [they] reject the cultural captivity of Jesus depicted by Euro-Americans."[23]

But why then, if Roberts was concerned about protecting Christ's universality, did he even present a model of a Black Christ? Even though he recognized the psychological need for Black people to see Christ as Black, was that enough for him to take the chance of Christ's becoming "overidentified" with a particular group of people?

If serving as a pastor of a church in the middle of riot-torn

Detroit compelled Cleage to call Jesus Black, and teaching at a white school outside Detroit during the riots helped move Cone to say something about Christ's Blackness, then teaching at a Black university in the midst of a major Black urban area compelled Roberts to do the same.

At the time of the Black Power and Black consciousness movement Roberts was teaching at Howard University. The students at Howard, like Black students on other college campuses, were affected by the Black Power/Black consciousness development.[24] In addition, Stokely Carmichael had been a student at Howard. As a Black theologian, Roberts could not teach in a Black university without addressing the concerns about Christianity and the White Christ, which were so poignantly raised by the young advocates of Black Power/Black consciousness. The Howard students certainly did not allow him to avoid these concerns. Roberts later acknowledged that the students at Howard were the primary reason why he developed an understanding of Christ from the Black experience of struggle.[25]

Like other Black theologians, Roberts was also called upon by the National Committee of Black Churchmen to give guidance in the development of a Black theology.[26] If, he explained, he was not to become "alienated" from the Black church and theological community, he had to say something about "what it means to be at once black and Christian in the United States."[27]

In general, Roberts's acknowledgment of Christ's particularity was a response to the demands placed upon him by his own particularity. To maintain his theological integrity at Howard as well as within the Black religious community, he had to present some understanding of Christ as Black. To maintain his theological integrity with the wider world community with which he identified intellectually, he had to protect Christ's universality. Roberts's version of the Black Christ, therefore, pointed not just to a paradox of the incarnation, but also to a paradox in his own life.

Given the three very different versions of the Black Christ, what in general can be said about the meaning of Black in relation to Christ? In spite of their different emphases, all three interpretations stated that Christ was Black. To call Christ Black in a White racist society pronounced that the racists were wrong—Blackness was not a color to be abhorred, since even the divine took it on. To call Christ Black also revealed that to be a Black and Christian did not necessitate submission to a White Christ. Finally, each interpretation of the Blackness of Christ announced to the White church and theological community that a proper understanding of Christ must confront Christ's Blackness.

THE SIGNIFICANCE OF LIBERATION AND RECONCILIATION

Calling Christ Black not only meant that Christ affirmed Black people in their Blackness, but also that Christ identified with the Black struggle to be free. Cleage, Cone, and Roberts understood Christ's identification with the Black liberation struggle in different ways.

Cleage's Version

Because Cleage argued that Christ was literally Black, he was able to interpret Christ's identification with the contemporary Black struggle as a part of a long history of God's attempts to build an independent Black nation. Cleage divided this history into at least three distinct time periods: the time of the exodus, the time of Jesus, and the time of Malcolm X.

The exodus time was characterized by the Israelites' escape from Egyptian bondage. Cleage recognized that the Black God chose the lowly Israelites, who of course were a Black people, in an attempt to build them into an independent Black nation. God took the first step toward building this Black nation by delivering the Israelites from their Egyptian oppressors into the promised land. After the Israelites received their freedom, Cleage said they turned away from the teaching of their Black God. They became corrupt and distracted from God's will. They did not act together to build an independent Black nation. They fought each other in attempts to gain individual power. Cleage described the early Israelite situation this way:

A people who had once been a Nation, who had been delivered from bondage in Egypt, who had wandered for forty years in the wilderness, who had fought their way into a promised land, this people had degenerated into a mass of individuals who no longer had any sense of a Nation. Each individual was willing to sell out the Nation for personal gain.[28]

Although the Israelites had turned away from God, Cleage pointed out that God did not turn away from them. God sent Jesus to redeem the Black nation. Jesus' entrance into Israelites' lives marked the second period of the Black nation's history— the time of Jesus.

Jesus' time was characterized by attempts to free the Israelite nation from Roman rule. Cleage explained: "Jesus was the non-white leader of a non-white people struggling for national liberation against the rule of a white nation, Rome."[29] Cleage specifically identified Jesus with the Zealots, a revolutionary group that had "spurred" numerous rebellions against Rome. As a Zealot, Jesus attempted to "rebuild [the Israelite] Nation out of . . . fragmented individuals."[30] Jesus was crucified because the Romans feared that Jesus would succeed in uniting the Israelites, and thus succeed in disrupting the Roman Empire.

According to Cleage, Jesus' time did not end abruptly with the crucifixion. It continued with the resurrection. The resurrection, Cleage argued, was not something that happened to Jesus. The notion that Jesus rose from the dead as a sign of a good life in heaven was, according to Cleage, a "lie" perpetuated by White slaveholding Christianity to distract Black people from their earthly situation. Cleage described the resurrection as the revival of Jesus' ministry after his death. It was marked by the disciples' attempts to carry forth Jesus' vision of building a Black nation:

[The Disciples] were not primarily concerned with the Resurrection of Jesus as an individual. Jesus had taught that a Black Nation was to come into being out of a people who had ceased to believe in the possibilities of a new Nation and his Disciples had begun to catch a glimpse of this kind of Resurrection.[31]

Unfortunately, according to Cleage, the resurrection did not result in an unbroken commitment to build a Black nation. Like the early Israelites, Black people again lapsed. In the twentieth century, therefore, Black people were fragmented and fighting against one another for power within the White nation. This continued until Jesus' goal for a Black nation was resurrected by Malcolm X.

Malcolm's time was similar to Jesus' time. Both Malcolm and Jesus "tried to bring black people together, tried to give them a sense of purpose, and to build a Black Nation."[32] Cleage further argued that "the things which Brother Malcolm X taught, Jesus taught two thousand years ago."[33] Malcolm's teachings involved identifying the Black nation's enemy as "the White man" and recognizing that Black people had to gain power in order to become an independent Black nation. The success of the Black nation in twentieth-century America, Cleage explained, depended upon "the total involvement of all black people, identification with black people, accountability to black people, and the severing of any identification with white people."[34]

Given the history of the Black nation—which stretched from the exodus to Malcolm X—what then was the Black Christ's meaning for the contemporary Black liberation struggle? The Black Jesus was the historical link between the contemporary Black community and the early Israelites. The Black Christ allowed Black people to know that they were the nation the Black God chose to bring to freedom. The Black Christ suggested that as God's people, Black people's primary, if not only, concern should be for their freedom as an independent Black nation.

Cone's Version

Similar to Cleage, Cone argued that the Black Christ was thoroughly committed to the liberation of Black people. Also like Cleage, Cone viewed the Black Christ's commitment to Black liberation as part of a long history of God's commitment to the Black oppressed. Cone too linked Black people's history to the early Israelite history. But unlike Cleage, he did not link the Israelites and Black people genealogically. Again, he made an existential connection.

Cone's understanding of the relationship between the Israelites and the Black oppressed was informed by slave Christianity. Whereas Cleage considered slaveholding Christianity normative for the Black church, Cone recognized slave Christianity as normative. Consequently, Cone did not have to discredit the Black Christian tradition, as did Cleage, in his effort to declare that Christ was a liberator for Black people. He utilized that tradition as a source for his claims about the Black Christ. Reflective of slave Christianity, the exodus event and the events of the cross were interpretive keys for Cone's articulation of the Black Christ's significance for the contemporary Black freedom struggle.

For Cone, the exodus event had at least two main components: God's deliverance of the Israelites from Egyptian bondage and God's election of the Israelites as God's people. Cone argued that the Old Testament did not make it entirely clear why God chose the Israelites. One point, however, was made clear: God's election of the Israelites was related to their oppressed condition and God's liberating activity on their behalf. Cone pointed out that God's deliverance of the Israelites was the basis for their covenant with God at Sinai:

> You have seen with your own eyes what I did to Egypt, and how I carried you on eagle's wings and brought you here to me. If only you will listen to me and keep my covenant, then out of all you peoples you shall become my possessions.[35]

Cone concluded that the exodus event revealed God as "the God of history whose will is identical with the liberation of the oppressed from social and political bondage."[36] To further substantiate his claims that God was a liberator of the oppressed, Cone pointed out that later in Israel's history, God raised up prophets to speak against oppression within the Israelite community.

Cone went on to argue, similarly to Cleage, that Jesus Christ came to fulfill God's covenant with the Israelites. He explained:

"In order to keep the divine promise to make Israel 'a kingdom of priests and a holy nation' . . . [God] became a Jew in Jesus of Nazareth."[37]

If Jesus was a Jew who came to help free the Jews and to make them into a nation, what allowed Cone to say that Christ was a liberator of the Black oppressed? Cleage was able to call Christ a liberator of Black people because he said the Jewish nation was a Black nation. Israelite history and Black history were the same, in Cleage's understanding. Cone did not recognize them as the same. It was the events of the cross that provided Cone with a way to make a connection between what Jesus did for the Israelites and Christ's contemporary concern for Black people.

According to Cone, the crucifixion and resurrection transformed Jesus' liberating ministry to a particular oppressed group into a liberating ministry for all those who were oppressed. The crucifixion, Cone explained, substantiated the particularity of Jesus' liberating ministry:

> The cross of Jesus is God invading the human situation as the Elected One who takes Israel's place as the Suffering Servant and thus reveals the divine willingness to suffer in order that humanity might be fully liberated.[38]

The resurrection revealed that Jesus' liberating ministry was not restricted to first-century Jews. First, it disclosed the universality of Jesus' liberation. Cone said: "the resurrection is God's conquest of oppression and injustice, disclosing that the divine freedom revealed in Israel's history is now available to all."[39] Second, that Christ was resurrected meant that Christ was raised from the dead and was not confined to the first century. Christ transcended history and was present in contemporary society.

While Cleage did not make a distinction between the Jesus of history and the Christ of faith, Cone did. Based on the recognition that Christ existed beyond the first-century Jew, Cone was able to affirm Christ's presence in the contemporary Black freedom struggle. What then did he suggest about the Black

Christ's significance for Black people as they struggled to become free?

Consistent with his view that the resurrection universalized Christ's liberating ministry, Cone could not identify Christ with any movement that might suggest that Christ's liberating concern was exclusive to a particular group of people. Yet, consistent with his view that in a White racist society Christ was Black, Cone had to identify Christ with a movement that had Black freedom from White racism as its primary goal. He put it sharply:

> If Jesus Christ is in fact the Liberator whose resurrection is the guarantee that he is present with us today, then he must be black, taking upon his person and work the blackness of our existence and revealing to us what is necessary in our destruction of whiteness.[40]

Cone identified the Black Christ, not with Malcolm X, but with the Black Power movement that Malcolm X spawned. He stridently explained:

> Black Power, even in its most radical expression, is not the antithesis of Christianity, nor is it a heretical idea to be tolerated with painful forbearance. It is rather, Christ's central message to twentieth century America.[41]

Roberts's Version

Like Cleage and Cone, Roberts' understanding of Christ's significance to the Black freedom struggle was informed by God's relationship to the early Israelites. Similar to Cone, Roberts made an existential, not genealogical, connection between the Israelites and Black people. But while Cone emphasized their common oppression, Roberts emphasized their common status as redemptive sufferers. For Roberts, being a redemptive sufferer carried a special ethical responsibility for reconciliation. The exodus event and the ministry of Jesus Christ were the keys for understanding the exact nature of this responsibility.

Roberts's interpretation of the exodus event focused on

God's election of the Israelites. He agreed with Cone that this election was unrelated to Cleage's notion of God and the Israelites sharing a common ethnicity. Yet, his understanding of the Israelites' election encompassed more than Cone's oppression/liberation motif. Roberts argued that God chose the Israelites not just to reveal that God was a liberator of the oppressed, but primarily to reveal that those who suffered unjustly were called by God to carry forth a mission of reconciliation. The Israelites, were chosen to transform their "unmerited" suffering as a vehicle toward reconciliation. Careful not to suggest that the oppressed must suffer always, Roberts argued that reconciliation required that the oppressed become liberated. He explained:

> A people chosen of God is a people who have entered into a new understanding of their mission in the world. Instead of being victims of suffering, such people transmute suffering into a victory. It becomes a rod in their hand to enter into a redemptive mission among themselves and others. . . . Upon entering into a deeper understanding of how their own lives have been purged and purified by unmerited suffering, they become a "saving minority," for all men.[42]

Roberts developed his argument further by recognizing, similar to Cone and Cleage, that the exodus provided "a central category for interpreting . . . the work of Jesus. . . . "[43] He said that Jesus Christ also revealed the importance of redemptive suffering for the manifestation of God's reconciliation. As with Cone's, Roberts's understanding of Jesus Christ's significance hinged on a distinction between the Jesus of history and the Christ of faith. While Cone suggested that the Jesus of history and Christ of faith corresponded with one another in terms of their ministry, Roberts suggested that they were in tension with each other. Similar to Cone, he contended that the Jesus of history particularized the gospel message, while the Christ of faith universalized it. But, unlike Cone, Roberts interpreted Jesus' particular interest as different from Christ's universal interest. He argued that Jesus revealed God's concern for the liberation of the oppressed, while Christ revealed God's concern for the reconciliation of all people to each other. Roberts proclaimed that Jesus meant freedom, but Christ meant reconciliation. The question for him was how to "reconcile the scandal of particularity [liberation] with the universalism of the gospel [reconciliation]."[44] The cross provided Roberts with a means to do this.

Roberts acknowledged that Jesus' cross, like his birth and ministry, identified him with the liberation of the oppressed. But he also recognized that on the cross Christ endured unmerited suffering so that humanity might experience God's reconciliation — that is Christ endured the crucifixion for the sake of the resurrection. Roberts concluded, "Christ is Reconciler and the ministry of the cross is reconciliation."[45]

Given the primacy of redemptive suffering for the purpose of reconciliation in Roberts's understanding of Christ's meaning, what is the Black Christ's significance for the Black freedom struggle? According to Roberts, the reconciling Christ called all people to be reconciling agents in the world. Black people, like the Israelites, were especially called because of their experience of unmerited suffering:

> Black Christians have borne their cross through the years. They know the meaning of unmerited suffering. They can now carry on a ministry of reconciliation across the generations and between races and nations — and become agents of healing in a broken world.[46]

If God chose Black people to carry on a "ministry of reconciliation," what were the implications for the contemporary Black freedom struggle? Although Roberts did not join Cleage and Cone in making a one-to-one link between Christ and a particular segment of the Black movement, he was clear about who best embodied Christ's reconciling ministry — Martin Luther King, Jr. Roberts pointed out that King was properly concerned, not just with liberation, but with reconciliation between Blacks and Whites. Roberts explained, "Dr. King . . . had a firm grasp of Biblical ethics — one that will win in the long run."[47]

While Cleage and Cone did not ignore the Black Christ's concern for reconciliation, they did not interpret the significance of reconciliation in the same way that Roberts did. Cleage argued that Christ's reconciling message was not a call for Black people to become reconciled with White people, but a critique of internal relationships within the Black community. He said that the Black Christ challenged Black people to become united as a people so that they could become an independent Black nation.[48]

Cone suggested on numerous occasions that Roberts misunderstood the meaning of Christian reconciliation.[49] He explained that reconciliation was primarily an act of God, which God effected through Christ: "God was in Christ reconciling the world to himself."[50] He described God's reconciliation as destruction of all the oppressive "principalities and powers" that separated humanity from God as well as from each other. With particular reference to Black people's oppression, Cone said that God's reconciliation meant "destroying all forms of slavery and oppression in White America so that people of color can affirm the authenticity of their political freedom."[51] Cone concluded that Black people's response to God's reconciling activity should not be a specific concern to become reconciled with White people, but a concern to become liberated from White racism.

Given the diversity of claims concerning Christ's message of liberation and reconciliation, what then does it mean to identify Christ with the Black freedom struggle? It refuted any notions that Christ supported, either through silence or direct action, White racist oppression. All three interpretations confirmed that Christ supported Black people in their struggles against White racism. The difference between the three interpretations was the degree to which Christ was concerned exclusively with Black people's liberation as well as the particular freedom movement with which the Black Christ was identified.

VIOLENCE OR NONVIOLENCE?

The question now is how far would the Black Christ go in supporting the rights of Black people to be free? What did the three versions of the Black Christ have to say about the means for liberation? Did the Black Christ support the right of self-defense? Did the Black Christ allow Black people the option of utilizing violence to secure their freedom?

The answers to these questions were especially important during the 1960s Black freedom struggles. The use of violence became one of the rhetorical concerns of White church and political leaders. While they rarely spoke about the violence of a White racist society, they often spoke out against what they saw as "violent" tactics used by Black freedom fighters. They essentially denied Black people the right to self-defense in their encounters with the violently hostile responses of White resisters to Black freedom. Vocal White church and political leaders made clear that they preferred the "turn the other cheek" philosophy of Martin Luther King, Jr., as opposed to the "by-any-means necessary" philosophy of Malcolm X. They revealed their position toward Black people's use of any kind of retaliatory or defensive violence when they often counseled them, after some of the most hideously violent acts carried out against the Black community, to use "restraint" in their responses.[52]

What did Black theologians say about violence? Did the Black Christ compel Black people to "turn the other cheek" or allow for Black people to use "any means necessary" to protect and nurture Black life? Again Cleage, Cone, and Roberts provided three different answers.

Cleage's Answer

Although Cleage did not directly advocate violence, his version of the Black Christ strongly affirmed self-defense and in so doing suggested that violence was not only appropriate for self-defense, but perhaps the most appropriate method of protest. Cleage's position concerning the use of violence is most clearly demonstrated in his comments surrounding Martin King's assassination.

Cleage claimed that the fact that King, an advocate of nonviolence, was assassinated demonstrated that nonviolence was unacceptable in the fight against White racism. He put it sharply:

If Dr. King's death proved anything beyond a shadow of a doubt, it proved that non-violence will never work in a violent white racist society . . . he tried in every way possible to be nonviolent. He took no steps to protect his life. . . . He hoped, and he prayed, that the black man's nonviolence could somehow redeem white people. He believed it. And you know what white people did to him? They killed him![53]

Cleage was so profoundly concerned about Black lives that he refused to endorse any philosophy that handicapped Black people in protecting themselves. How did he reconcile his concern to protect Black lives with the Black Christ? How did he account for Jesus' admonition to "turn the other cheek"?

As mentioned earlier, Cleage claimed that Jesus, the Black Christ, was a member of the Zealots. He also acknowledged that the Zealots were a revolutionary group responsible for several rebellions against the Roman Empire. Cleage's association of the Black Christ with the Zealots indicated Cleage's belief that the Black Christ did not condemn, and perhaps even preferred, the use of violence as a means for overthrowing a White racist regime.

Consistent with his belief that Jesus was concerned to develop a united Black nation, Cleage argued that the "turn the other cheek" demand was directed toward members of the Black nation in relationship to each other:

Jesus didn't spend all of his time walking around talking about love. He was trying to bring the Nation together. When he said, "Go the second mile, turn the other cheek," he meant inside the Black Nation. When he said, "Don't come to the altar and try to pray unless you've made peace with your brother," he was talking about inside the Nation.[54]

Essentially, while Cleage was careful not to directly advocate violence, his concern for self-defense and his strong reactions against nonviolence implied that violence was a viable option if Black people were to gain their freedom.

Cone's Answer

Cone argued that the Black Christ prescribed neither violence or nonviolence as a liberation strategy. In making his argument, Cone maintained his crucial distinction between the Christ of faith and the Jesus of history. Cone said that the Christ of faith, "the resurrected Christ," was not restricted to first-century possibilities. The actions of the Black Christ were not limited to a "slavish imitation" of the actions of the Jewish man from Nazareth. To be sure, Jesus' actions were a guide for understanding what the Black Christ was doing in contemporary society. But the importance of Jesus' actions was not in the *details* of what Jesus did. It was in the *meaning* of what he did. Jesus' actions indicated a commitment to the liberation of the oppressed. The Black Christ should carry forth Jesus' liberating ministry to the oppressed.

What then did the Black Christ suggest about the use of violence or nonviolence in the Black liberation struggle? According to Cone's understanding, the Black Christ's primary concern was for Black people's freedom. It did not prescribe a particular strategy to effect this freedom. A Black Christian was challenged by the Black Christ to fight for liberation without knowing exactly what Jesus would have done in any given situation. This was what Cone called an unavoidable risk of faith:

> But the gospel of Jesus means liberation; and one essential element of that liberation is the existential burden of making decisions about human liberation without being completely sure what Jesus did or would do. This is the risk of faith.[55]

In practice, Cone's understanding of what the Black Christ suggested about the use of violence translated into Black Power's "by-any-means necessary" philosophy. This philosophy was concerned with efficacy—that is, the best method to assure the liberation of Black people. Whereas most people, especially White people, assumed that "by-any-means necessary" was synonymous with violence, it was not. This philosophy simply meant that violence was not eliminated as an alternative for fighting the violent oppression of White racism.

Cone's version of the Black Christ allowed Black Christians freedom to choose the most appropriate method for achieving their liberation. They were not limited to first-century standards or restricted by what their White oppressors, who of course regularly used violence to keep them oppressed, considered acceptable standards of action.

Roberts's Answer

While Cleage's Black Christ strongly supported violence, and Cone's allowed for violence, Roberts's precluded violence. Roberts argued that Christ's universal concern for reconciliation eliminated violence as a possible strategy for achieving Black freedom.

Roberts explained that violence might lead to Black people's liberation. It, however, did not lead to Black and White reconciliation. Roberts put it this way:

> Violence that destroys the one who is party to the reconciliation is not a good means. . . . Violence may offer some promise for those who seek only liberation for blacks. . . . But the "whole gospel" in race relations must never rest with separation as an end in itself. The black man is not to be liberated and separated, but liberated and reconciled.[56]

Roberts's stance on violence was consistent with his emphasis on Christ's identification with all of humanity. If Christ were only Black, and thus only promoted Black liberation, then the Black Christ might accept violence as a possibility. Since the Black Christ was the universal Christ who promoted reconciliation, then only nonviolence would be acceptable to the Black Christ. Roberts summarized his position: "the nonviolent revolution offers reconciliation beyond confrontation and liberation of the oppressed. This I envisage as a proper Christian goal."[57]

To summarize, what did the Black Christ mean for a Black people in struggle against White racist oppression? In all three versions, to call Christ Black indicated that Christ was for Black freedom and against White oppression. Any representation of Christ that suggested otherwise was a distortion of the gospel witness to Christ. Although the three versions varied in their explanations of Christ's Blackness, the important point was that Black theologians had clearly spoken. They made it clear that freedom-seeking Black people did not have to say, "To Hell with Christianity and its Jesus." Declaring that Christ was Black let it be known that Christ had profound meaning for a people determined to be free and proud of their Blackness.

What can be said now about Black churchgoers' and seminarians' responses (as referred to earlier) to each of these versions? First, they correctly perceive the very different challenges that each model presents. Cleage's Black Christ is the only one that challenges Christians to accept Jesus as an African. The appeal to Black Christians of Jesus' being African apparently overshadows the other aspects of Cleage's version, which is less accepting of the White community than Cone's. Thus, they tend to ignore the other features of Cleage's Black Jesus while celebrating Cleage's claims concerning Jesus' ancestry.

Cone's version challenges those who are not on the side of the oppressed. He is strident in his claim that Christ, hence the Black Christ, is where Black people are struggling for their freedom. To be for Black freedom is to be with Christ, but to be against, or even neutral, in relation to the Black freedom struggle is to be of the antichrist. It is this straightforward claim concerning Christ's unambiguous commitment that Black churchgoers seem to resist. What they do not seem to understand, however, is that Cone's version of the Black Christ is not exclusive. All people, Black and White, can receive salvation from Christ if they accept the challenge to meet Christ in the struggle for freedom.

Black Christians rightly perceive Roberts's version of the Black Christ as one that emphasizes reconciliation. This version appears to appeal to their desire not to alienate the White community. Left to determine, regardless of the current perceptions of Black churchgoers and seminarians, is the effectiveness of each of these versions. This will be explored in the next chapter.

Chapter 4

A CRITICAL ASSESSMENT
OF THE BLACK CHRIST

Black theologians' declaration that Christ was Black was a definite response to a particular theological crisis. During the 1960s, Black Americans were passionately engaged in a fight for their humanity. They needed to know, in no uncertain terms, if Jesus Christ was for or against them. There was no room for ambiguity. Either Jesus supported their struggle for respect and freedom, or he did not. At stake was the integrity of Black people's Christian identity. Was Christianity a compromise to Blackness?

Black theologians stridently answered no when they pronounced that Christ was Black. They let freedom-seeking Black people know that Christianity and Blackness were not incompatible. By calling Christ Black, Black theologians responded to the challenge before them.

Was calling Christ Black the best way to make clear that the Christian God was for Black people? Did the Black Christ adequately represent Christ's meaning for the Black community? This chapter will attempt to assess the adequateness of the claim "Christ is Black" for a Black people with their minds "stayed on freedom."

Before looking at the effectiveness of the Black Christ in general, it is important to evaluate the claims made by each theologian. Were Cleage's, Cone's, and Roberts's explanations of Christ's Blackness persuasive?

AN ASSESSMENT OF EACH CLAIM

Cleage's Black Christ

Although other Black theologians often quoted Cleage's claims that Jesus was literally Black in order to "shake up" White Christians, they were reluctant to argue that Jesus had a genealogical relationship to Black Americans.[1] Cleage observed that Black theologians "were willing to assert the relevance of the Black experience [for a proper understanding of the Christian gospel] without coming to grips with the historic fact that Jesus was a Black man."[2] Black theologians thought Cleage went beyond the available historical evidence in his conclusions about Jesus' Blackness. J. Deotis Roberts voiced strong opposition to Cleage's claims when he said, "[Cleage] has done violence to biblical history without scholarly justification."[3]

Were Cleage's claims erroneous? Did he "do violence" to biblical history? Was Jesus of Nazareth a Black man?

Other Black religious scholars acknowledged that though they did not have the proper support for such a claim, Cleage was on the right track when he argued for Jesus' Blackness. They made it clear that given Jesus' geographic origins, he probably looked more like Black Americans than White Americans. To be sure, he was not Aryan in appearance.[4] Twenty-one years later historical and biblical scholarship affirms that Cleage was on the right track. There is now evidence to support his claim that Jesus was dark-skinned and that the early Israelite tribes to which Jesus was ancestrally linked were a mixed group of people with African connections.[5] Cleage's claims were only weakened by his attempts to access Jesus' ancestry through the biblical genealogies.

Cleage based his conclusions that Jesus was of African heritage and an ancestor of Black Americans, in part, on information provided by the Matthean genealogy. Some biblical scholars have argued that given the inconsistency between Matthew's genealogy and the one provided by Luke, it is inappropriate to use either as a means for gathering accurate information about Jesus' heritage. Biblical scholars have noted that both genealogies "have in the long run been fashioned by the evangelist to serve a special function," which perhaps mitigated the need to provide an accurate family tree for Jesus.[6]

Though biblical scholarship may not have supported Cleage's usage of Matthew's genealogy, the significance of his project is not undermined. With the tool of his trade as a preacher, the Bible, Cleage took a bold step in rescuing Jesus from the racist biases of White biblical scholarship. He challenged the long history of Western scholarship that "whitenized" Christian symbols, even Jesus.[7] He took risks that other Black theologians were not willing to take. He did not concern himself with respectability in the White academy. He was concerned to provide a means for Black Christians to gain self-respect. He wanted them to be able to see themselves, not their oppressor, in the face of Jesus. Cleage's Black African Jesus accomplished this objective.

As acknowledged in the previous chapter, Cleage's version of the Black Messiah continues to be a source of pride and excitement for young Black churchgoers. It often motivates them to explore further the possibilities of Jesus' ancestry. Whether or not Cleage went beyond the evidence he had available to him when he called Jesus Black, is not important. What is important is that after Cleage Jesus could not be seen in the same way: as a White man. He freed Jesus from the limitations of a White racist society. He invalidated any claims that Jesus looked like White Americans. Most importantly, he clarified the need for Black religious scholars to more thoroughly explore what it meant in terms of ancestral heritage for Jesus to be a Jew from Nazareth.

Roberts's Black Christ

Roberts's affirmation of Christ's Blackness was based almost entirely on the fact of the incarnation. In an effort to call Christ Black without jeopardizing Christ's identification with all people, Roberts focused on God's act of becoming incarnate. He said that in becoming Christ, God identified with all humanity. Because of Christ's universal identification with humanity, Roberts concluded that Christ could be *any* color that represented a segment of humanity.

To suggest that Christ can be any color of humanity is inconsistent with Jesus' unequivocal identification with the oppressed and nullifies Christ's Blackness. Jesus' life disclosed that he was one with the oppressed in their efforts to survive and be free from that which oppressed them. Jesus' birth, ministry, death, and resurrection revealed his unambiguous identification with the socially downtrodden in their struggle against injustice. By concentrating on the universality of the incarnation, Roberts trivialized the particularity of Jesus' earthly existence. He developed an understanding of Christ that was contradictory to Jesus' identification with the oppressed.

Because Jesus as Christ identified with all humanity, Roberts conceded that Christ could be White. To call Christ "White" in a society where to be White is to be identified with oppressors, identifies Christ as an oppressor. A White Christ undercuts Jesus' identification with the oppressed.

A White Christ also nullifies Christ's affirmation of Blackness. If Christ is White, then he affirms that which "shames Black people in their Blackness" — Whiteness. Roberts's focus on the incarnation at the expense of Jesus' ministry allows for a Christ who is Black, but does not allow for a Christ who definitively affirms Blackness. It does not prevent Black people from being "shamed" by a White Christ.

Roberts's understanding of the Black Christ also results in a negation of Christ's commitment to the Black freedom struggle. This is evidenced in Roberts's emphasis on Christ's commitment to reconciliation.

Roberts did not deny Jesus' liberating ministry. But he continued to trivialize the importance of this ministry in his emphasis on reconciliation. For instance, he interpreted the events of the cross as the culmination of the incarnation as opposed to the climax of Jesus' earthly ministry. He said that through the crucifixion and resurrection, the universal Christ revealed a primary concern to reconcile all humanity to God as well as to each other. This emphasis on reconciliation has the potential to negate Christ's concern for liberation. This is most clearly illustrated in Roberts's discussion on violence.

Roberts suggested that the Black Christ supported the Black struggle to be free only if that struggle did not involve Black people's use of violence. Violence might lead to Black liberation, Roberts argued, but it might not lead to reconciliation between Whites and Blacks. If the liberation struggle — for whatever reason — necessitated the use of violent tactics, then the implication of Roberts's argument is that Christ would not support it. Christ's concern for White/Black reconciliation seems to outweigh Christ's concern for Black liberation. An even more interesting aspect of Roberts's argument is that he questioned Black people's use of violence without questioning the violence of White oppression.

Because Roberts's Black Christ was more concerned with Blacks and Whites becoming reconciled than with Black people becoming free, it did not adequately respond to the challenges of the 1960s. This was not a Christ who clearly identified with Black people in their struggle to be free. In spite of the acceptance that this version of the Black Christ may have with Black churchgoers, especially those who enjoy "privileges" from the civil rights movement, this Christ could not empower or liberate the masses of Black people who still experience the most insidious effects of a racist society. Simply put, Roberts's Black Christ does not take a definitive stand for Black freedom.

Cone's Black Christ

Cone's version of the Black Christ was based on an analysis that emphasized a compatibility between the Jesus of history and the Christ of faith — that is, Christ's contemporary presence. Christ's meaning was not limited to the historical Jesus, although the historical Jesus was the authoritative guide for understanding Christ. With Cone's analysis it was not necessary to determine the details of Jesus' ministry. It was only important to discern the nature of his ministry.

Cone concluded that Jesus' ministry was characterized by its focus on the liberation of the oppressed. This ministry to the oppressed was the governing principle for discerning Christ's contemporary presence. It was the basis for Cone's calling Christ Black.

The claim that Christ was Black was grounded on the fact that Jesus identified with the oppressed. Cone concluded that since Black people were the oppressed ones in twentieth-century America, Christ was Black. The implication of this argument was that Christ could not be a color of humanity that signified oppressors, but only a color that signified the oppressed. In White racist America, Christ could not be White. This version of the Black Christ has much to commend it.

First, Cone's understanding of the Black Christ takes seriously slaveholding Christianity. It draws upon Black Christian tradition as it makes its claims about Christ. In doing so, it reveals the historical viability of Christianity for Black people struggling to survive and be free. It releases Christianity from the misconceptions of being a religion suited only for the oppressor or for those willing to passively accept their earthly condition in hope for a better life in the "bye and bye."

Second, by using the Black religious experience as such a prominent source for discerning Christ's Blackness, Cone let it be known that the Black experience of struggle provided valuable insight for understanding God's meaning in human history. His strident articulation of a Black Christ made clear that the Black story of suffering and struggle was God's story, and this was a story necessary to tell. Cone essentially rescued Christ from the confines of a White history of dominance.

Third, Cone's Black Christ disclosed that a proper understanding of the Christian gospel had to take seriously those who were marginalized and oppressed. It prevented the White religious and theological community from remaining silent with impunity about the Black plight. If they continued to ignore the Black condition, they would — at the least — have to deal with the claims that Cone so stridently made about the essence of the Christian message and hence the essence of Jesus Christ.

Clearly, Cone's version of the Black Christ freed Black people from the shame of worshiping a White Christ. It affirmed not only Blackness, but also the Black experience of struggle in White racist America. What it did not do was take the risk of naming the historical Jesus "Black." While it forthrightly emphasized Christ's Black American identity, it avoided a discussion of Jesus' African identity.

It was who Jesus was, White or Black, that was the issue for Black nationalists such as Malcolm X. To circumvent the color of the historical Jesus by emphasizing the Blackness of the Christ of faith sidesteps Malcolm's most poignant critique of Christianity: that it is founded upon a White Jesus. Whether or not it would answer to all the objections of a Malcolm X or other Black nationalists, attention must be given to Jesus' color as well as his ancestral heritage. The most thorough and effective version of the Black Christ is one that confronts the Blackness of the historical Jesus, as well as the Christ of faith.

IS THE BLACK CHRIST ADEQUATE?

While calling Christ Black certainly responded to the challenges of the 1960s, one question still remains. Does calling Christ "Black" adequately indicate Christ's significance for the Black community? Is the Black Christ, as it emerged in Black theology, one who is truly a liberator and empowerer of the Black community? The answers to these questions suggest some major weaknesses, shared by all three versions of the Black Christ, which would render the Black Christ ineffective for Black people as they seek dignity and freedom.

Lack of Internal Critique

The strength of the Black Christ is that it embraces Black people in their Blackness. It avows not only what it means to be physically Black, but also Black experience, heritage, and culture. It fosters a sense of self-esteem and pride in Black people as they come to understand that who they are is not abhorred, but valued by the divine being. They are able to see themselves in Christ. This very strength, however, is also a weakness.

While Black theologians attempted to affirm Blackness by identifying Christ as Black, they seemed to do so unconditionally. They did not sufficiently specify what it was that Christ affirmed, in affirming Blackness. Not everything that is Black is sustaining or liberating for the Black community. There are aspects of Black culture and religion that do not necessarily foster self-esteem, nor do they empower Black people to fight for their freedom. "Blackness" must involve more than just being a particular color, or being of a particular ethnic group, or identifying with a particular cultural and historical experience. It must include an ethical concern and commitment to the well-being and freedom of all Black people. That means that everything that comes from Black people or is a part of the Black life is not acceptable. It is not "Black." If one is to identify Christ as Black, it is important to clarify precisely what that entails, otherwise the Black Christ may not be a sustaining and liberating Christ.

Further, by calling Christ Black, Black theologians clearly responded to the need to identify Christ as one who opposes White racism. The Black Christ explicitly disavows White oppression of Black people. The problem is that it does not go beyond that. It does not portray the complexity of Black oppression. Specifically, it does not address the fact that Black people oppress each other, and that racism is not the only barrier to Black freedom.

The various versions of the Black Christ do not confront the reality of oppression *within* the Black community. The Black Christ does not point to the reality of Black on Black oppression. Black people are victimized not only by White people, but also by each other. The Black community and church is often divided against itself over many different issues. For instance, the "haves" in the Black community—the middle class—often look down upon the "have nots"—the poor. The middle class too often harbors a sense of resentment toward the poor. A spirit of "pull yourself up by your own bootstraps" prevails over a spirit to help those who remain trapped in the vicious cycle of poverty. Black people are left divided against themselves.

What does the Black Christ say to those Blacks who were to some extent "integrated" into White racist political-economic structures, as a result of the Civil Rights/Black Power movement, and who vigilantly protect their positions within those structures, even at the expense of other Black people? How does the Black Christ challenge those Black people who look down on other Black people who have not "made it" in White racist America? Merely identifying Christ as Black does not indicate Christ's relationship to Black people as they discriminate against each other. The Black Christ does not readily challenge Black people to free themselves from the various forms of oppression within the Black community. It does not obviously compel Black people to look at the ways in which they enslave themselves or perpetuate enslaving structures and systems. Essentially, calling Christ Black does not prod Black people to become a "whole" community as it struggles for freedom.

One-Dimensional Analysis

In addition to ignoring the oppression *within* the Black community, calling Christ Black does not acknowledge that skin color is not the only barrier to Black liberation. Racism is not the only form of persecution visited upon the Black community. Black people live in a society that is also sexist, classist, and heterosexist. There are persons in the Black community who suffer and are discriminated against because of their gender, economic status, or sexual preference. Calling Christ Black explicitly indicates Christ's opposition to White racism, but it is not apparent that it is concerned with eradicating other forms of oppression. The Black Christ appears impervious to any kind of discrimination beyond White racism. A Christ who is only concerned with abolishing White racism is ineffectual for those whose lives are marred by more than just White racism. A Black Christ does not sustain and liberate the entire Black community.

Essentially, the Black Christ was such a thorough response to the 1960s Black freedom struggles that it was impotent in dealing with concerns beyond racism. It, like the movement that called it forth, was grounded in a social analysis focused on race. The Black Christ signaled a one-dimensional understanding of social oppression.

The Failure of the Black Christ to Impact the Black Church

Though the Black Christ was born out of Black faith, it ironically has not made significant inroads in Black churches. As mentioned in the Introduction, many Black churches continue to display images of a White Christ. Various suggestions have been made concerning why the Black Christ has had apparently little impact on Black churches. These reasons basically point to shortcomings of Black theology itself.

Gayraud Wilmore has argued that the reason Black theology "is failing to reach [Black] pastors and congregations" . . . is because "it has ceased to harmonize the radical message of Black liberation with the more conservative message of healing and self-fulfilment through a saving faith in Jesus Christ."[8] Essentially, Wilmore argues that if Black theology and its Black Christ are to have an impact on Black churches, they must concentrate not just on the fight against social-political injustice, but also on the pastoral concerns of Black Christians. It must, Wilmore explains, be both political and pastoral. It must seek "to read the signs of the times to discover what God is doing with individuals trapped in the misery of personal sins, and communities trapped in worldly structures that oppose ethnic self-determination and encourage cultural suicide."[9] It is only with this kind of political-pastoral emphasis, says Wilmore, that Black theology and the Black Christ can have any meaningful influence on Black churches.

Cornel West makes a similiar observation as he argues that liberation theology — Black theology — has failed to deal with the spiritual and personal aspects of Christian faith.[10] Pastor and theologian Dennis Wiley recognizes similiar limitations of Black theology as those put forth by West and Wilmore. He suggests, however, that many of these limitations are an effect of Black theology's being too far removed from Black churches. He argues that Black theology has become too identified with the academy — universities and seminaries — at the expense of its identification with the Black church. He laments a gap between the Black theologians and Black pastors. In order for Black theology, and hence the Black Christ, to have a greater impact on Black churches, Wiley says that this gap must be closed.[11]

While Wilmore, West, and Wiley may be correct in their identification of Black theology's various shortcomings in relation to the Black church, they tend to overlook the inherent problem with any prophetic theology such as Black theology. "A prophet is not welcome in his or her own home." If Black theology is truly prophetic in the Black church—thereby challenging its business as usual—then it is not likely to be popular within that church. Yet the prophetic edge of Black theology still does not explain the Black Christ's limited impact in Black churches. There is perhaps an even more significant factor in the failure of the Black Christ to have a meaningful impact on Black churchgoers. This lack of impact signals an even more egregious limitation. In calling Christ Black, Black theologians did not take seriously the experiences of more than half of the Black church and community.

The Failure to Acknowledge Black Women

Not one of the three versions of the Black Christ acknowledged the presence or role of Black women in the Black community's struggle for dignity and freedom. Perhaps if they had done so, some of the previously mentioned limitations could have been avoided.

Just as they have been a part of the historical struggle for Black survival and Black liberation, Black women were a significant part of the Civil Rights/Black Power movement out of which the Black Christ emerged. They, like Black men, went to jail, were beaten, and put their lives on the line for Black freedom. They helped found two of the most significant Civil Rights organizations and led some of the most notable protests. For instance, it was after Ella Baker prodded Martin Luther King, Jr., about follow-up to the 1956–57 Montgomery bus boycott that he was moved to form The Southern Christian Leadership Conference (SCLC). It was also Ella Baker who called college students from across the country to a conference at Shaw University (Raleigh, North Carolina) in April 1960. It was as a result of this conference that SNCC was formed.

It was Gloria Richardson who, during this civil rights era, organized the first grassroots protest against the segregation of public accommodations to take place out of the Southern United States, the 1962 Cambridge, Massachusetts, Movement. And certainly without the efforts of Fannie Lou Hamer, the Mississippi Freedom Democratic Party would never have been formed. It was she who led the delegates from this group to the 1964

Atlantic City Democratic Convention, where under her leadership they mounted a campaign to be seated as the official delegation from Mississippi.

Beyond the more public figures like Baker, Richardson, or Hamer, there were also the Joann Robinsons, Diane Nashs, Unita Blackwells, Annie Mae Kings, Ruby Doris Smiths, Emma Jenkins, and scores of other black women who made significant contributions to the civil rights and Black consciousness movements.

As Black women gave tirelessly to the Black freedom struggle, it became clear that a significant segment of the Black community was plagued by more than White racism. Black women suffered under the yoke of gender exploitation as well as racial oppression.

Regardless of the pivotal roles that they played, Black women were never accorded the same treatment or respect as their Black male colleagues. The very organizations that nurtured the Civil Rights/Black Power movement, and which Black women helped to create, made it appallingly clear that Black women were not considered equals to Black men. Black women were rarely afforded the opportunity to hold national leadership roles or even be national spokespersons for these various organizations. The 1963 March on Washington poignantly illustrates the oppressive treatment of Black women during the contemporary Black freedom struggles.

The organizers of the march carefully enlisted participation from almost every faction represented in the struggle for social justice, including women from other ethnic groups. But until a week before the march, they had not invited a single Black woman to speak. As Anna Arnold Hedgeman pointed out, not even SNCC, an organization characterized in some ways by its very active Black female participation, acknowledged the need for Black women to take part in the March program.[12] Not until Hedgeman wrote a letter of protest to one of the march organizers, A. Philip Randolph, were Black women asked to sit on the dais. Even then, Black women were barely acknowledged. Hedgeman recounted the events of that day:

> Wryly, it occurred to me that women, too, were not adequately included in man's journey toward humanity. Rosa

Parks was presented . . . but only casually, in spite of the fact that she was the pioneer of this phase of the struggle for freedom. Daisy Bates . . . was given only a few moments in front of the microphone.[13]

As significant as Black women were to the contemporary Black struggle, and as obvious as their discriminatory treatment was, what accounts for the failure of Black theologians to even acknowledge their existence? Why did all three versions of the Black Christ ignore Black women's reality?

The answer to this question may in part be reflected in the fact that Black women did not draw attention to their peculiar experience. During the 1960s Black freedom struggles they did not articulate consistently or with clarity the complexity of their oppression. They did not explicitly identify the reality of sexism as they encountered it.

There were of course many reasons for Black women's failure to name their unique oppression as women. Many considered sexism an issue raised by White women to subvert the Black freedom movement. Others felt that the time had come for Black men to assert their manhood in a White racist society, which had deprived them of doing so. In general, both Black women and men believed that the Black community was better served if Black women supported Black men in the battle against White racism. Black women expressed this conviction in various ways. One Black woman said, "We should stand behind our men, not against them."[14] Prominent literary artists voiced similar sentiments. Nikki Giovanni commented:

I think that [sexism is] a moot issue. . . . Just another attempt of white people to find out what black people are doing or to control what we are doing . . . black people consider their first reality to be black, and given that reality we know from birth that we are going to be oppressed — man, woman, or eunuch![15]

Gwendolyn Brooks joined the chorus:

Black women, like all women, certainly want, and are entitled to, equal pay and privileges. But black women have a

second "twoness." Today's black men, at last flamingly
assertive and proud, need their black women beside them,
not organizing against them.[16]

These comments reflect, in part, Black women's own ambiv-
alence in regard to asserting themselves as women. Their loyalty
to the Black community as a whole prevented them from advanc-
ing their rights as equal participants in the Black struggle.[17]
Their failure to assert themselves no doubt contributed to Black
theologians' inability to recognize the importance of Black wom-
en's experience for determining Christ's meaning for Black people. Yet this was not the only contributing factor, and possibly
not the most significant. Perhaps an even more influential cause
was Black theologians' myopic visions.

Cleage, Cone, and Roberts were not unlike other Black men
during that period. They too had been socialized into a sexist
society. They too were victims of that socialization. They harbored sexist attitudes and saw the world through sexist lenses.
As men they were not constrained to take women seriously. They
too adopted the language and attitudes of men seeking "manhood" within sexist parameters.[18]

Those who proclaimed that Christ was Black were blinded by
their maleness. Their peculiarity as men prevented them from
appreciating vital facets of Jesus' ministry. The male Jesus who
was able to reject the privileges of being male in a patriarchal
world was lost on these theologians. They, for instance, did not
comprehend the story of Jesus and the Syrophoenician woman
(Matthew 15:21–28). In this story, Jesus, apparently controlled
by the biases of his society, which considered Syrophonecians
and especially women untouchable creatures, harshly rebuffs the
woman's pleas for help. It is not until after the woman reminds
Jesus that "even the dogs eat the crumbs that fall from the
master's table," that Jesus realizes how he had succumbed to
the privileges of being Jewish and male in that particular society.
With this apparent realization, Jesus rejects the validity of those
privileges by helping the woman. This story could have become
a model for Black theologians to move beyond the advantages
of maleness and to have taken seriously the reality of Black
women. But this aspect of Jesus' ministry was not recognized by

these theologians. Consequently, they remained focused solely on the concerns of racist oppression, as they were understood from a Black male perspective. This inability to move beyond their maleness to consider Black women's lives profoundly contributed to their one-dimensional understandings of what it meant for Christ to be Black.

THE EMERGENCE OF WOMANIST THEOLOGY

As a result of Black women recognizing the contradiction of participating in freedom-fighting organizations, which actively discriminated against them, and as Black men continued to display blatant sexist attitudes and behaviors, what can now be called a "womanist" consciousness began to emerge.[19] Black women started to articulate the unique oppression connected to being both Black and female in the United States. Works such as Ntozake Shange's *For Colored Girls Who Have Considered Suicide When the Rainbow IS Enuf* and Toni Cade's *Black Woman* appeared. These books revealed the complexity of Black women's reality. Black women enlisted such terms as "slave of a slave," or "double jeopardy" to point to what it meant to be an oppressed member of an already oppressed group. With the emerging "womanist consciousness" Black women began to openly discuss their experiences as Black women and to search for ways in which to gain their freedom without becoming alienated from the Black community as a whole — particularly Black men.

It is as part of this developing consciousness of what it means to be Black and woman that a womanist theology has emerged. Black women began to recognize that it was not just within secular organizations and within the Black community in general that they were discriminated against. It was also in the Black church. If the experience of being Black and woman can generally be described as a "double jeopardy," Black church-woman Theressa Hoover described the experience of Black women in the church as a "triple jeopardy." Black women have addressed the contradiction involved in a church that espouses a belief in a Jesus Christ who is liberator of the oppressed, yet oppresses its own membership. For instance, many Black churches continue to refuse Black women ordination. Further,

Black women have consistently questioned why the Black church is not reflective of the fact that at least 75% of the Black congregants are female. Recent statistics suggest that Black women constitute less than 5% of Black church and denominational leadership.[20]

As Black women began to critique the Black church, they also began to critique Black theology. Jacquelyn Grant provided the earliest critique of Black theology in her 1979 article, "Black Theology and the Black Woman."[21] In this article she recognized that by ignoring the experiences of Black women, Black theologians rendered Black women invisible in their theologies. Grant ended her 1979 assessment by charging that with Black women representing more than 50% of the Black community and more than 70% of the Black church, no "authentic theology of liberation [can] arise out of those communities without specifically addressing the liberation of women in both places." Finally, Grant challenged Black women to continue to name their experience of oppression and "to keep the issue of sexism going in the Black community, in the Black church and in Black Theology until it has been eliminated."

It is in keeping with Grant's charge that a "womanist understanding" of Jesus Christ is emerging. As pointed out earlier in this chapter, the Black Christ is inadequate for understanding the meaning of Jesus Christ for a community besieged by more than just White racism. It cannot address the complexity of Black women's oppression. Womanist theologians are now engaged in developing a theology and understanding of Jesus Christ that is more reflective of the interest of the entire Black community.

It should be noted, however, that it is not just the failure of Black theology that has compelled the development of a womanist approach to Christ. Feminist theology has also contributed to this development. In order to fully appreciate the distinctiveness of a womanist portrayal of Christ it is necessary, before leaving this chapter, to take a brief look at the limitations of feminist theology in relationship to Black women.

Feminist Theology and Black Women

Feminist theology emerged as a part of the "women's" liberation movements in America. This theology's biases, especially as they affect its import for Black women, mirrors the biases of these movements. bell hooks aptly characterized the American women's movement when she pronounced, "Every women's movement in America from its earliest origin to the present day has been built on a racist foundation."[22]

Essentially, the first distinctive women's movement in American evolved out of abolitionism. This nineteenth-century movement found women fighting for the right to vote. The contemporary women's movement likewise emerged out of the 1960s Black freedom struggle. This movement found women demanding freedom from their exile in the domestic realm and equal access to the male-dominated social-political realm. Undergirding both movements was a struggle against patriarchalism. Patriarchalism was based on Victorian ideology, which considered women—that is, White women—fragile dolls who had to be placed upon protective pedestals. They were consequently relegated to the home and prevented entrance into the public arena.

Neither movement acknowledged that Black women's lives were an antithesis to Victorian ideology. Neither movement recognized the difference that race makes in relationship to patriarchalism. Consequently, racial bias distinguished both movements as they neglected the concerns of Black women.[23]

Unfortunately, the theological manifestation of the contemporary women's movement, feminist theology, also disclosed a neglect of Black women. Black women have vigorously critiqued feminist theology for its exclusion of their experience. One of the earliest critiques of feminist theology was an open letter by Audre Lorde addressed to Mary Daly. Lorde pointed out that Daly's particular book, *gyn/Ecology*, excludes Black women's heritage from its descriptions of women's religious experience.[24] The power of Lorde's observation was revealed in her words:

> So, the question arises in my mind, Mary, do you ever really read the work of black women? Did you ever really read my words, or did you merely finger through them for quotations which you thought might valuably support an already conceived idea concerning some old and distorted connection between us.[25]

In addition to her penetrating questions, Lorde pointed out that by ignoring Black women's experience, Daly perpetuated "the racism and separation between women."[26]

Delores Williams has been the most strident and unrelenting in her critique of feminist theology. In an article where she also criticized Black theology, Williams observed that White feminists have failed to consider the history of the relationship between White and Black women. She challenged White feminist theologians to make an analysis of women's relational history integral to any discussion of women's oppression so that oppression of women at the hands of other women is not overlooked.[27]

Williams's most notable critique was a response to an article by Rosemary Ruether, "Feminist Theology in the Academy."[28] In this article Ruether described various developmental stages of feminist theology and then predicted its future within seminaries and universities. Williams responded to Ruether's article by pointing out that since Ruether consistently ignored Black women and did not clarify that she was speaking only for White women, her claims were "as exclusive and imperialistic as the Christian patriarchy she opposes."[29]

Feminist theologian's one-dimensional focus on White women's reality has also manifested itself in their understandings of Jesus Christ's significance for women. They have been concerned to show Christ's identification with the struggle against patriarchalism. They have drawn attention to Christ's maleness and attempted to resolve the tension created by a male savior for women. They asked if, in a patriarchal society, a male savior could save women? Rosemary Ruether answered this by pointing out that in spite of his gender, Jesus defied all hierarchal systems that set one group of people over another, specifically men over women.[30] Mary Daly has moved beyond Christianity because she has found the problems attached to the maleness of Jesus insurmountable.[31]

Though feminist theologians such as Ruether and Daly have claimed to develop christologies that are concerned with "women's" liberation in church and society, Jacquelyn Grant has noted that like feminist theology in general, feminist christology overlooks Black women's concerns.[32]

The parallels between Black theology and feminist theology in relationship to Black women are striking. Both emerged as a part of liberation movements that were primarily concerned with one dimension of social oppression. In adopting the one-dimensional focus of these movements, both theologies failed to adequately address Black women's multidimensional oppression. Consequently, both have developed understandings of Christ that do not necessarily reflect Black women's experience. In this regard, both have contributed to the emergence of womanist approaches to Christ. The next chapter explores a womanist perspective on Christ, specifically on the Black Christ.

Chapter 5

A WOMANIST APPROACH TO THE BLACK CHRIST

LAYING A WOMANIST FOUNDATION

While the Black Christ of Black theology does not signal an appreciation of Black women's experience, a womanist understanding of the Blackness of Christ begins with the Black woman's story of struggle. This portrayal of Christ reflects at least two aspects of that story: the multidimensionality of Black women's oppression and their determined efforts to survive and be free from that oppression. Specifically, a womanist portrayal of Christ confronts Black women's struggles within the wider society as well as within the Black community. It also affirms Black women's steadfast faith that God supports them in their fight for survival and freedom. Such an understanding of Christ emerges as womanist theology engages a social-political analysis of wholeness and a religio-cultural analysis.

A Social-Political Analysis of Wholeness

As was discussed earlier, during the 1960s freedom struggles Black women were reluctant to assert their rights as women. Many refused to join the contemporary woman's movement in its fight against sexism, because they believed it would alienate them from Black men. They did not want to participate in any movement that had even the potential of creating hostilities and divisions between them and their men. This hesitancy to claim their own unique experience and to advance their own cause for freedom is characteristic of Black women's historical struggle.

Black women have traditionally been concerned, not just for their welfare, but for the welfare of their entire community and families—sons and daughters, husbands and brothers. Alice Walker points to this aspect of Black women's lives when she describes a womanist as one who is "committed to the survival and wholeness of entire people."[1] No person in history better illustrates this womanist commitment than does Harriet Tubman. After her own successful escape to the North from slavery, Tubman returned to rescue her family. She continued to make trips back to the South, at great peril to her own life, to lead other slaves to freedom. Walker points to Tubman's story when, as a part of her womanist definition, she relates the following dialogue: " 'Mama, I'm walking to Canada and I'm taking you and a bunch of other slaves with me.' Reply: 'It wouldn't be the first time.' "[2]

As a result of their consistent commitment to their families and their community, Black women have searched for a "politics" of wholeness as they have evaluated their participation in various freedom movements, such as the contemporary woman's movement and the 1960s Black freedom struggle. These women needed a political strategy that would assure Black people, men and women, rights to live as whole, free, human beings and that would keep the Black community whole, unified, in striving for liberation. Reflective of this particular concern, a womanist theology includes a social-political analysis of wholeness.

This analysis is multidimensional and bifocal. That means that it seeks to understand how race, gender, class, and sexual oppression interact in the persecution of Black people, especially Black women. It may, for instance, be informed by Marxist thought as it endeavors to understand the class issues within the Black community. But it also goes beyond Marxist analysis in an effort to comprehend the multidimensionality of Black oppression. Moreover, unlike Marxist analysis, a social-political analysis of wholeness takes seriously the particularities of race, gender, and culture that shape the nature of Black people's oppression.

As it is bifocal, a social-political analysis of wholeness will confront racism, sexism, classism, and heterosexism not only as they impinge upon the Black community, but also as they are nurtured within that community. It addresses the ways in which the Black community and Black institutions—that is, church, schools—perpetuate Black oppression. It does not seek to prioritize different forms of oppression, or to pit women against men/the poor against the rich. It does, however, seek to eliminate anything that prevents Black people from being whole, liberated people, and from living and working together as a whole, unified community. For instance, this analysis of wholeness might challenge the "haves" in the Black community who maintain their status by supporting structures of oppression. It will confront the alienation that often develops between the Black middle class and the Black poor.

But perhaps more importantly, a social-political analysis of wholeness challenges womanist scholars to forthrightly confront heterosexism within the Black church and community. With the exception of women's full ordination, no issue has caused more discussion in the Black church than that of sexuality. With AIDS rising to epidemic proportions in the Black community, this discussion has been unavoidable. Some Black church ministers routinely preach from their pulpits that AIDS is a "disease visited by God upon homosexuals because of their sinful lifestyle." During a recent workshop I conducted with Black ministers, they voiced their hesitancy to minister to those inflicted with AIDS, in spite of the gospel dictum for them to care for the sick (Matthew 25:44f.). Their reluctance was clearly related to their homophobia. They stridently argued that "homosexual" practices (of course they believed that homosexuals were the primary carriers of this disease though this is increasingly not the case in the Black community) were unnatural and went "against the way and will of God." They were even more passionate in their claims that gay and lesbian lifestyles were a threat to the stability of the Black family.

One of the most divisive and explosive issues in womanist theology courses I have taught has been sexuality. I have often been surprised to discover that Black women, in spite of their own sense of marginalization due to gender and race, have been most strident in their antagonism toward gay and lesbian people. They have frequently shown the same intense homophobia displayed by the Black ministers described above.

Unfortunately, womanist theologians and other womanist religious scholars have been slow to engage the sexuality issue. Many of us, when utilizing Walker's womanist definition, have ignored Walker's reference to a womanist as "a woman who loves other women, sexually and/or nonsexually."[3] One who did not ignore this reference was ethicist Cheryl Sanders.

In a 1989 roundtable discussion in the *Journal of Feminist Studies in Religion*, Sanders objected to Black female religious scholars adopting the womanist concept. She argued that given the "context, criteria and claims" of Walker's definition, it is incompatible with Christian theological and ethical principles. Sanders's primary objection was Walker's apparent affirmation of the lesbian lifestyle. Sanders forthrightly states:

> In my view there is a discrepancy between the womanist criteria that would affirm and/or advocate homosexual practice, and the ethical norms the black church might employ to promote the survival and wholeness of black families. It is problematic for those of us who claim connectedness to and concern for the black family and church to engage these criteria authoritatively and/or uncritically in the formulation of theological-ethical discourse for those two institutions. If black women's ethics is to be pertinent to the needs of our community, then at least some of us must be in a position to offer intellectual guidance to the church as the principal (and perhaps only remaining) advocate for marriage and family in the black community. There is a great need for the black churches to promote a positive sexual ethics within the black community as one means of responding to the growing normalization of the single-parent family, and the attendant increases in poverty, welfare dependency, and a host of other problems. Moreover, it is indisputably in the best interest of black children for the church not only to strengthen and support existing families, but also to educate them ethically for marriage and parenthood. The

womanist nomenclature, however, conveys a sexual ethics that is ambivalent at best with respect to the value of heterosexual monogamy within the black community.[4]

Though Sanders's statement shows clear disdain for gay/lesbian lifestyles, and though it posits homosexuality as a major threat to the Black "family" structure, the womanist respondents to her article did not directly confront these issues. They challenged Sanders's interpretation of the womanist nomenclature, but they did not dispute the homophobic implications of her statements. Womanist religious scholars missed a perfect opportunity to denounce heterosexism as a part of "an interlocking system of race, gender, class and sexual oppression."[5]

Sociologist Patricia Hill Collins has acknowledged Black women's, particularly Black feminists' such as womanists', silence on heterosexism. She makes two poignant observations in this regard. First, she recognizes Black women's desire to hold on to their heterosexual privilege. She argues: "In the same way that that white feminists identify with their victimization as women yet ignore the privilege that racism grants them, and that Black men decry racism yet see sexism as less objectionable, African-American women may perceive their own race and gender oppression, yet victimize someone else by invoking the benefits of heterosexual privilege."[6] Second, Collins points out that silence concerning homosexuality shields Black women from becoming a part of the "ultimate other" in relation to the heterosexual, White, male norm. She pointedly says: "Another reason Black women have been silenced about Black lesbian relationships concerns the traditional treatment in Eurocentric thought of the lesbian as the ultimate other."[7]

A social-political analysis of wholeness compels womanist theologians to break the silence. It requires us to "audaciously" denounce heterosexism as it is present in the Black church and Black community, as well as in womanist religious scholarship. Womanist scholars are constrained to confront our tendency to enjoy "heterosexual privilege." We must make clear that homophobia in any form is unacceptable, and that heterosexism must be eradicated as it is a part of the same interlocking system of race, gender, and class oppression. If womanist theologians con-

tinue to maintain silence concerning the oppression of our lesbian sisters, not only do we perpetuate their oppression, but we
fall far short of our own vision for wholeness.

A social-political analysis of wholeness also challenges the
Black community to move toward "wholeness" not only as a
community, but also in relationship to other oppressed communities, especially people of color around the world. This analysis will prompt Black people to confront the history that divides
them from other oppressed people as well as to recognize the
history that links them.

More particularly, a social-political analysis of wholeness
encourages womanist theologians to continue their dialogue
with Third World women of color. This dialogue currently takes
place primarily within the context of the Ecumenical Association
of Third World Theologians (EATWOT). Initially, the relationship between the womanist theologians (at the time the only
women who were a part of the U.S. minority delegation) and
the other EATWOT women was strained. The most clear
instance of this occurred at the EATWOT's 1986 second general
assembly held in Oaxtepec, Mexico. A week prior to this assembly, women from Asia, Africa, and Latin America met in order
to share experiences, to express their mutual concern for the
elimination of gender oppression, and to plan for a meeting with
North American feminist theologians.[8] Black American women
were not invited to be a part of this week-long meeting. Black
American women's exclusion appeared to be, in part, an outgrowth of the long EATWOT struggle to understand the role of
First World minorities in a Third World organization. The
EATWOT women of the Third World had accepted an organ-
izational procedure for their preconference, which, perhaps
unwittingly, resulted in the marginalization and oppression of
some of their womanist sisters.

During the meeting of the second general assembly, an over-
ture was made to U.S. Black women. It was made, however, as
a step toward meeting with White feminist theologians of the
First World. The women of Asia, Africa, and Latin America had
already accepted an invitation to dialogue with North American
feminists. They reasoned that it would be beneficial to meet with
Black American women first, since it was we who had the most

experience of and interaction with these feminists. At this point in our time together I began to wonder if the women from Asia, Africa, and Latin America were more interested in those who had contributed to their oppression than in getting to know their sisters in oppression.

A social-political analysis of wholeness makes clear that if Third World women are going to move toward a world community where gender oppression is eliminated, we cannot accept, for whatever reasons, the kinds of structures and systems that keep us separated from each other. If we are truly committed to the struggles of our sisters, we must forge links with each other whether we are Third World women living in Third World countries or Third World women trapped in the First World. It is only together that we will be able to free our churches and society from the evils of race, class, gender, and sexual oppression that keep our sisters in bondage. A social-political analysis of wholeness consistently challenges various divisive and alienating structures of oppression whether they are part of church, society, or the organizations in which women are a part. Sojourner Truth put it best when she said:

> If the first woman God ever made was strong enough to turn the world upside down all alone, these women together ought to be able to turn it back, and get it right side up again.[9]

It is *together* that Third World women will be able to turn the world right side up again.

Fortunately, by week's end of the second general assembly, EATWOT women from the Third and First World were united in the desire to get to know more about one another. The dialogue with First World feminists was postponed until after Asian, African, Latin American, and U.S. minority women could dialogue. This conversation took place at a week-long conference held in 1988 at the Interdenominational Theological Center (Atlanta, Georgia). At this conference we explored our commonalities and differences. We forthrightly confronted the divisions between us, and committed ourselves to strengthing the links that bind us. We agreed that it was only in concert that we could make a difference in the lives of our oppressed sisters around the world. Today, our solidarity continues as we now prepare as one for a dialogue with First World feminists. A social-political analysis of wholeness urges womanist scholars to remain in solidarity with their oppressed sisters around the world. It seeks a world where all women, indeed all humanity, live together in relationships of mutuality. It is grounded in the dictum that "No woman is free, if all—that is, men and women—are not free."

Finally, and perhaps most fundamentally, a social-political analysis of wholeness recognizes the importance of wholeness for the individual as well as the community. This analysis urges Black people, but especially Black women, to confront the ways in which societal oppression has left them less than whole beings—spiritually, emotionally, psychologically, and so forth. The underlying assumption is that only individuals who are at least moving toward wholeness can nurture wholeness within the community.

A Religio-Cultural Analysis

A womanist understanding of the Black Christ also begins with a religio-cultural analysis. This analysis lifts up those aspects of Black life—that is, of Black religion and culture—that are sustaining and liberating for Black people. It also disavows those aspects of Black life that do not nurture survival and liberation. A religio-cultural analysis recognizes that not everything "Black" necessarily benefits the Black community. For instance, in twenty-five years the Black community has come full circle in terms of its need to affirm Blackness. What was once labeled "Black consciousness" can now be seen in the call for Afrocentrism. The Afrocentric concern attempts to trace the roots, especially African roots, of African-American culture in an effort to nurture self-esteem and cultural pride in African Americans. A religio-cultural analysis would challenge those involved with the Afrocentric project to critically evaluate what they unearth, to recognize that just because something is African or Black does not signify that it has value for Black people as they move toward wholeness. A more specific example may illustrate the point.

Black culture has recently given birth to "rap" music. While a religio-cultural analysis will affirm rap music as an important cultural expression, especially for young Black people, it will disavow those forms of rap music that perpetuate abuse of women and other destructive behaviors or images. These kinds of negative images create division, not wholeness, in the Black community.

In regard to Black religion, a religio-cultural analysis challenges any aspects of Black faith that perpetuate the discrimination of particular segments of the Black community. For instance, the ways in which the Black church uses the Bible in the oppression of women, gays, and lesbians will be confronted.

While a religio-cultural analysis recognizes that there are enslaving and divisive aspects of Black religion and culture that must be repudiated, it also recognizes that there are sustaining and liberating aspects that must be confirmed.

A religio-cultural analysis attempts to highlight that which has allowed Black women to transcend the negative, dehumanizing images that society has maintained of them. It lifts up that which has undergirded their fight, against all odds, to save their children from the tyrannies of a society that seeks to destroy Black life. It affirms that which Black women, who have traditionally been the purveyors of culture and religion in the Black community, have handed down to their children in order to facilitate their survival. Essentially, a religio-cultural analysis assumes the presence of a "spirituality of resistance," which Black women have nurtured and passed on to their sons and daughters.[10]

There are at least two aspects of this spirituality of resistance. It provides a sense of heritage, and it nurtures a connectedness to God. The words of nineteenth-century Black female freedom fighter, Maria Stewart, often illustrate the characteristic features of a spirituality of resistance. During one of her exhortations she reminded her Black audience about their rich African heritage:

> History informs us that we sprung from one of the most
> learned nations of the whole earth, from the seat, if not

the parent, of science. Yes, poor despised Africa was once the resort of sages and legislators of other nations, was esteemed the school for learning, and the most illustrious men in Greece flocked thither for instruction.[11]

She also frequently reminded her audiences that though the world considered them inferior, God did not. She told them that they were children of God, made in God's own image. She put it this way:

Many think, because your skins are tinged with a sable hue, that you are an inferior race of beings, but God does not consider you as such. He [sic] hath formed and fashioned you in his [sic] own glorious image, and hath bestowed upon you reason and strong powers of intellect.[12]

A spirituality of resistance implies, as Stewart apparently understood, that if an oppressed people have a pride in their own culture and historical heritage, as well as a knowledge that they are children of God, then they will not be as vulnerable to the oppressive structures, systems, and ideologies that attempt to convince them that they are nobody, and that their lives are not worth living. An essential task of a religio-cultural analysis is to accent those aspects of Black religion and culture that contribute to this spirituality of resistance.

SOMETHING *MORE* ABOUT THE BLACKNESS OF CHRIST

So what does all of this mean for the Black Christ? Given the significance of a social-political analysis of wholeness and a religio-cultural analysis for a womanist approach to understanding Christ's relevance for the Black community, what can we say about the meaning of Christ for Black women and men?

Christ Is Black

It first must be understood that the primary concern in a womanist approach to Christ is not the fact of Christ's Blackness. In this regard, womanist theology affirms that for the Black community, Christ is Black. That is to say, Christ has Black skin and features and is committed to the Black community's struggle for life and wholeness. To assert the Blackness of Christ reflects Black women's unwavering commitment to their families and community, as maintained by a social-political analysis of wholeness. Such an assertion also continues to affirm the need for Black people to be able to see themselves in the image of Christ. It is, however, at the point of establishing more than the color of Christ that womanist theology goes beyond what has previously been said by Black theologians.

The Womanist Black Christ: More than an Endorsement of the Black Community

Reflecting the need for the Black community to be free from internal oppression as well as oppression visited upon it by the wider society, the womanist Black Christ does more than endorse Black people in their struggle against White racism. The womanist Christ is seen not just as sustainer and liberator – as presented in Black theology – but also as a prophet. A womanist approach to the Black Christ brings together, for instance, the images of Christ present in slave Christianity with those perpetuated by Martin King, Jr. That is, Christ is understood as carrying forth the work of Moses and Amos.[13] Christ is present in the Black community working to sustain as well as to deliver it from the multidimensional oppression that besets it. Christ is also present as a prophet, challenging the Black community to rid itself of anything that divides it against itself and to renounce any way in which it oppresses others.

The Womanist Black Christ: A Black Woman?

How do we point to this liberating and prophetic presence within the Black community? What does Christ look like? What symbols and icons can we use to capture the significance of Christ for Black men and women as they fight for dignity and freedom?

It is important to understand that symbols and icons are essential tools for pointing to the reality of Christ, and for helping people to see themselves in Christ and Christ in themselves.[14] Yet, it should also be understood that no *one* symbol or icon can capture the presence or meaning of Christ. Symbols and icons also need to change as the community changes, and attempts to discern Christ's involvement in their changing life situations. How is it that womanist theology can portray this sustaining, liberating, and prophetic Black Christ which eludes simple, static, depiction?

A womanist portrayal of the Black Christ avails itself of a diversity of symbols and icons. These symbols and icons are living symbols and icons as Christ is a living Christ. That is, womanist portrayals of the Black Christ endeavor to lift up those persons, especially Black women, who are a part of the Black past and present, who have worked to move the Black community toward wholeness. These portrayals of Christ suggest, for instance, that Christ can be seen in the face of a Sojourner Truth, a Harriet Tubman, or a Fannie Lou Hamer, as each one struggled to help the entire Black community survive and become whole. Seeing Christ in the faces of those who were and are actively committed to the "wholeness" of the Black community suggests several things.

First, it says that the Black Christ is present in the Black community wherever people are engaged in a struggle for that community's "wholeness." Second, it challenges Black people to participate in activities that advance the unity and freedom of their community. It allows them to know that Christ is with them and in them anytime they promote life and wholeness for Black men and women. Third, to portray Christ in the face of Black heroines and heroes signals that it was not who Jesus was, particularly as a male, that made him Christ, but what he did. Essentially, Christ's biological characteristics have little significance to discerning Christ's sustaining, liberating, and prophetic presence.

In addition to highlighting the presence of Christ in those who work toward Black wholeness, a womanist Black Christ will consistently lift up the presence of Christ in the faces of the poorest Black women. These women, as an icon of Christ, are important reminders of accountability. Any theology of "survival and liberation/wholeness" that emerges from the Black community must be accountable to the least of these in that community. It is only in a commitment to insure the life and wholeness for the "least of these" that we can grasp the radicality of who the Black Christ is for all Black people.

To suggest that Christ can be seen in the faces of Black women is not entirely new. Womanist theologian Jacquelyn Grant has put forth a similiar understanding of Christ.[15] Taking her lead from Black women's faith, Grant emphasizes the importance of the biblical witness to Christ as well as Black women's own witness of Christ in their lives as the primary sources for discerning Christ's power and significance. In so doing, Grant too disavows the centrality of Jesus' maleness in determining what it meant for him to be Christ. She says that the important factors were his humanity and his liberating actions on behalf of the oppressed. Informed by Jarena Lee's confession that Jesus is a savior of both men and women, and by Sojourner Truth's faith that women had the power to save the world, Grant concludes that today "Christ, found in the experience of Black women, is a Black woman."[16]

The difference, however, between Grant's understanding of Christ as a Black woman and the version presented in this text begins with the analyses that help to shape them. Grant stresses the importance of a tridimensional analysis that encompasses race, gender, and class oppression. For her a liberating Christ must be one who stands against this tridimensional tyranny. My christological perspective is not limited to a tridimensional analysis. Instead, it stresses the need for a multidimensional and bifocal analysis that confronts all that oppresses the Black community as it impinges upon the community or is harbored within. This means that Christ is a sustainer, liberator, and prophet in the face of such evil as racism, sexism, classism, and heterosexism.

Moreover, while Grant affirms that Christ found in Black women's experience is a Black woman, I affirm that Christ is found where Black people, men as well as women, are struggling to bring the entire Black community to wholeness. While my womanist perspective highlights the significance of Christ found in the faces of Black women in struggle, especially poor Black women, it does not eliminate the possibility of Christ's being seen in the faces of Black men who also struggle for Black women's, and men's lives and wholeness. In this regard, Christ for the Black community can be a Black woman, but the presence of Christ is not restricted to Black women.

Finally, it needs to be stressed that the womanist Black Christ is found where there is at least a struggle for Black life and wholeness. This means that all that Black women and men engage in is not reflective of the presence of Christ. As suggested by the religio-cultural analysis, there are aspects of Black reality that lead to destruction and death. Such a reality, as it thwarts life and wholeness, is antagonistic to the presence of Christ. In this regard a womanist portrayal of the Black Christ avoids one of the dangers Delores Williams sees in various understandings of Christ's significance.

Williams argues that many Christian communities, including Black churches, teach "believers that sinful humankind has been redeemed because Jesus died on the cross in place of humans. . . . In this sense Jesus represents the ultimate surrogate figure standing in the place of someone else."[17] Such a belief is problematic for Black women, Williams says, since inhumane and denigrating patterns of voluntary and coercive surrogacy have been a part of their reality. An understanding of Christ that supports surrogacy, Williams rightly claims, cannot be liberating or life-affirming for Black women who need to be set free from oppressive forms of surrogacy. Williams further concludes that understandings of Jesus that focus on his role as a surrogate wrongly emphasize the importance of his death as opposed to the importance of his life — that is, his ministry. Williams aptly asserts that humanity's redemption is to be found in life, not death.

A womanist Black Christ indeed critiques any aspect of Black existence, such as various patterns of surrogacy, that do not affirm life and wholeness. And again, informed by Jesus' ministry, womanist theology emphasizes Christ's presence in the movement for Black life.

So, is Christ a Black woman? Yes, when Black women are acting to establish life and wholeness for the Black community.

Other Christological Implications

Another often asked question is whether or not womanists' understandings of Christ can be considered christology. Typically, what the questioner really wants to know is, "Do womanist understandings of Christ take into account the Nicene/Chalcedonian tradition?"

In general, to do christology is to attempt to discern and define what it means for Jesus to be Christ — that is, "The bearer of God's rule, the mediator of God's salvation."[18] But in the dominant Western theological tradition, christological formulations typically rely in some way on the Nicene/Chalcedonian confession. This confession is seen as a norm or significant source for what is said about Christ. It claims that Jesus is Christ because of his unique metaphysical make-up. This make-up renders him God incarnate and uniquely the divine/human encounter.

Are womanists doing christology? Yes, in the sense that we are attempting to discern, from the perspective of Black women in struggle, what it means for Jesus to be Christ. No, if doing christology means that the Nicene/Chalcedonian tradition must provide a norm or even a significant source for what we say about Jesus as Christ.

Womanist understandings of Christ emerge out of the Black Christian tradition. This is a tradition in which Black women and men confessed Jesus as Christ because of what he did during his time as well as in their own lives. They did not make this confession because of his metaphysical make-up. Those in the slave community, for instance, were most likely unaware of the Nicene/Chalcedonian tradition, just as are many Black Christians today. An example from my own journey illustrates the point.

When I first entered Union Theological Seminary, I firmly believed, as I do now, that Jesus was Christ. Yet I knew relatively little about the Nicene/Chalcedonian debates. Born and raised an Episcopalian, I could perfectly recite the Nicene creed, but I did not know what that had to do with Jesus being Christ. Reflective of my upbringing in the wider Black religious community, I believed that Jesus was Christ because of what he did for others, particularly the poor and oppressed. As I learned about the Nicene/Chalcedonian debates and statement of faith, I accepted it as a part of the wider Christian tradition and history. Though I no doubt have been influenced by its claims, I did not accept it as the basis for why Jesus was Christ. I did not make it an integral part of my own faith. As I have listened to and learned from Black church women and men, I have discovered that I am not alone in my appropriation of the Nicene/ Chalcedonian tradition. Black Christians tend not to consider it relevant to their own beliefs about Jesus.

Finally, there are aspects of the Nicene/Chalcedonian formulation that appear inconsistent with Jesus as he was presented in the Gospels. For instance, this formulation establishes that Jesus is Christ by focusing on God's act of becoming incarnate in him. In so doing, it diminishes the significance of Jesus' actions on earth. His ministry is virtually ignored. The formulation reads:

> We believe in one God, Father, Ruler of all, Maker of heaven and earth . . . And in one Lord Jesus Christ, the only-begotten Son of God, begotten from the Father before all ages . . . who for us human beings and for our salvation came down from heaven and was incarnate from the Holy Spirit and Mary the Virgin and became human; and was crucified for us under Pontius Pilate, and suffered, and was buried, and rose on the third day in accordance with the Scriptures.[19]

This confession of faith moves directly from the act of the incarnation to the crucifixion and resurrection. The implication is that what took place between Jesus' birth and resurrection — the bulk of the Gospels' reports of Jesus — is unrelated to what it means for Jesus to be the Christ. All that matters is that God entered the world through him. If Jesus did conduct a sustaining, liberating, and prophetic ministry, this would not significantly affect what it meant for him to be Christ.

In addition, to emphasize the uniqueness of Jesus' metaphysical nature as that which allows him to be Christ, makes what it means to be Christ inaccessible to ordinary Christians. There becomes little reason to strive to be an example of Christ in the world, because to be Christ requires a divine incarnation, which happened only in Jesus. By ignoring Jesus Christ's ministry and focusing on his "being," he is set apart above humanity.

He is seen as someone to be worshiped, believed in, but not followed or imitated.

A womanist understanding of the Black Christ avoids these shortcomings. It does not begin with abstract speculation of Jesus' metaphysical nature. Instead, it starts in history with Jesus' ministry as that is recorded in the Gospels. What Jesus did becomes the basis for what it means for him to be Christ. This makes Christ more accessible to ordinary Christians. Such a christological understanding encourages others to be an example of Christ in their own lives. That is, Christ can be seen in the faces of others, Black women and men, as they strive in their own historical context to promote life and wholeness.

What then is the place of the Nicene/Chalcedonian formulation in womanist christology? This formulation is seen as a part of a continuing tradition in which those who confess Jesus as Christ attempt to discern the meaning of that confession. It does not, however, have any normative significance as womanist theologians attempt to articulate Christ's meaning for the Black community.

THE WOMANIST BLACK CHRIST CHALLENGES WOMANISTS AND THE CHURCH

Methodological Implications

To say that Christ is seen in the faces of Black women struggling to bring their communities toward wholeness, and in particular in the faces of poor Black women, necessitates that womanist theology be done as a part of a process of "praxis" centered in the lives of these women. Womanist theologians must resist the urge to retreat behind the walls of seminaries and universities. The womanist Black Christ demands that we remain involved in the lives of "ordinary" Black women in the church and in community organizations and groups. This is crucial primarily because the wisdom gained from these women should eventually empower these very women in their struggle for life and wholeness. As Patricia Hill Collins explains, it is Black women's everyday "taken-for-granted" knowledge that womanist scholars should rearticulate in such a way that it "empowers African-American women and stimulates resistance."[20]

This further means that womanist theology is accountable to "ordinary" Black women in struggle. What womanist theologians say about Jesus Christ must make sense, "ring true," to these women. This presents two significant challenges for womanist theologians as we attempt to articulate the meaning of Christ.

First, a commitment to teaching womanist theology not just in seminaries and universities, but also in churches and community-based organizations and groups is essential. Appropriate pedagogies for teaching church and community-based women need to be developed as a part of the womanist theological praxis.[21] New ways to communicate and teach womanist theology that grow out of the various contexts in which Black women are a part have to be devised. No doubt, these pedagogies will emerge as womanist theologians become emersed in the varied lives and contexts of Black women. We will learn from Black women in struggle the best ways to give back to them that which we have gleaned from them. Essentially, it will be church and community-based women who will teach womanist theologians how to make theology more accessible.

Second, if it is church and community-based women to whom our theology is accountable, then our dialogues with each other must take place beyond the academy. Thus far, most of our public discussions concerning our theology have taken place in the context of the American Academy of Religion. Womanist symposiums have taken place in front of an academy audience composed of mostly White women and men. They have listened in on our debates as well as raised questions as we have worked through our theologies. This must change.

Our public discussions must move to the places where Black women are. They must take place within the context of the Black church and community. Black church and community-based women should be our primary audience. They should be our most significant interlocutors. This necessitates that womanist theologians create opportunities to debate and discuss their ideas where Black women in struggle are the main audience. Such opportunities provide another means to be accountable to the very women whom womanist theology claims to represent.

Implications for the Black Church

Perhaps the most obvious implication for Black churches is the challenge to remove icons and symbols that portray Christ as a blond-haired, blue-eyed male. Womanist theology takes seriously Malcolm X's observation that Black self-esteem is sabotaged by the worship of a White Christ. Womanist theology advocates that Black churches display, throughout their buildings, images of Black heroines and heroes, making these images just as prominent as were the images of White Christs. Moreover, time must be spent—beyond Black history month—pointing out and teaching how these Black people who have struggled for the community's survival and wholeness reflect what it means to be Christ in the world.

Just as womanist theologians must create opportunities to teach and share with Black church women and men, the Black church must create opportunities for womanist and other Black theologians to share with their congregations.

But the issue becomes, why should the churches be any more open now than they have been with Black theology in the past? Why would male Black church leadership give womanist theologians more opportunities to share with their congregations than they have given Black male theologians? Why should male Black church leadership, which is often closed to women's ordination or even presence in the pulpit, be open to what womanists have to say? What would motivate Black church leadership to cleanse their buildings and pulpits of their White male images of Christ?

The impetus for Black church leadership to change its images of Christ, as well as become more open to women's ministry is going to have to come from their congregations. These congregations, which are often over 70% female, will have to be the ones to demand a change. It is only as Black church women claim their voice and power—that is, their power as the primary financial resource and workers of the church—that the church will be changed. A demand for change can occur only as these Black church women are empowered to fight for their "wholeness" within their churches and communities.

The charge for womanist theologians is therefore great. We

must be vigilant in our efforts to teach and share with these women. We must take advantage of every opportunity, whether it is in the context of community-based programs or women's programs in the church. Womanist theology can impact the church only as much as it impacts the women in the pews. When Black church women find their voice and demand a church that empowers them and their families, then the Black church leadership will have to respond, or be willing to lose its most loyal and supportive constituency. Moreover, it is when Black women find their voice in the church and begin to move the church toward wholeness that the church will be truly filled with the presence of Christ. Christ will then be seen in the faces of those Black women.

THE BLACK CHRIST FROM A WOMANIST EYE

We have now come full circle, affirming what Malcolm X claimed some thirty years ago, that Christ is Black. But in affirming Malcolm's claims, and similiar claims before and after him, we do it with a womanist eye on what is required if the Black Christ is to compel the Black church to advance wholeness for Black women and men.

A vital and effective Black Christ must reflect the complexities of Black reality. A womanist Black Christ is one who can respond to those complexities—that is, the Black struggle to "make do and do better" in face of racist, sexist, classist, and heterosexist oppression. A womanist Black Christ avoids the myopic concern for White racism. At the same time a womanist Black Christ enables Black women and men, girls and boys, to see themselves in Christ and Christ in themselves.

As I now reflect on my grandmother's faith in Christ, I realize that the Christ in her life had to be one who understood more than just what it meant to live in a racist society. My grandmother's Christ was one whom she could talk to about the daily struggles of being poor, Black, and female. So, it is in this regard that I continue to learn from my grandmother's faith. Her faith in Christ's empowering presence suggests, at the very least, a womanist Black Christ. But most importantly, it is in the face of my grandmother, as she struggled to sustain herself and her family, that I can truly see Christ.

In Alice Walker's Pulitzer Prize winning novel, *The Color Purple*, one of her female characters, Shug Avery, reminds the main protagonist, Celie, that God is present inside her. Shug simply says, "Here's the thing. . . . The thing I believe. God is inside you and inside everybody else."[22] For a womanist Black Christ, "here's the thing," Christ is inside of my grandmother and other Black women and men as they fight for life and wholeness.

NOTES

INTRODUCTION

1. "The Playboy Interview: Malcolm X Speaks with Alex Haley" (May 1963).

2. The Afrocentric movement is an attempt to reestablish the centrality of the African historical and cultural heritage in the lives of African Americans. The term "Afrocentrism" was coined by Molefi Kete Asante, chair of the African American studies department at Temple University. He remains one of the most prolific and prominent scholars of the Afrocentric movement. It should be noted that many biblical, theological, and ethical scholars have adopted or are articulating the significance of the Afrocentric paradigm for their work. See, for instance, Cain Felder, "Out of Africa I Have Called My Son" in *The Other Side* (Nov.-Dec. 1992), 8–14; see also Cain Felder, *Troubling Biblical Waters: Race: Class, and Family* (Maryknoll, N.Y.: Orbis Books, 1989).

3. Felder, "Out of Africa," 11.

4. For instance, Archbishop Augustus Stallings of the Imani Temple, an African American Catholic Congregation in Washington, D.C., called for Black churches to burn their White Christs on Easter day, 1993.

5. James Cone, *A Black Theology of Liberation* (Philadelphia: Lippincott Press, 1970); 2nd ed. (Maryknoll, N.Y.: Orbis Books, 1986).

6. Cornel West, "The Black Church and Socialist Politics," in his *Prophetic Fragments* (Grand Rapids, Michigan: William B. Eerdmans; Trenton, New Jersey: Africa World Press, 1988), 67.

7. Ibid.

8. Kenny Moore, "Sportsman of the Year: The Eternal Example," in *Sports Illustrated* (December 21, 1992), 21.

9. Gayraud S. Wilmore and James H. Cone, eds., *Black Theology: A Documentary History, 1966–1979* (Maryknoll, New York: Orbis Books, 1979).

118

10. See, for instance, Gayraud Wilmore, "The Black Messiah: Revising the Color Symbolism of Western Christology," *Journal of the Interdenominational Theological Center* 2 (Fall 1974), 8–18; Major Jones, *Black Awareness: A Theology of Hope* (Nashville: Abingdon Press, 1971); *The Color of God: The Concept of God in Afro-American Thought* (Macon, Georgia: Mercer Press, 1987); William Eichelberger, "A Mytho-Historical Approach to the Black Messiah," idem, *Journal of Religious Thought* 33 (Spring-Summer 1976), 63–74; "Reflections on the Person and Personality of the Black Messiah," *The Black Church* vol. 2 no. 1 (Spring 1974), 51–63.

CHAPTER 1

1. *Ebony* (March 1969).

2. Vincent Harding, "Black Power and the American Christ," reprinted in Gayraud Wilmore and James Cone, eds., *Black Theology: Documentary History, 1966–1979* (Maryknoll, N.Y.: Orbis Books, 1979), 37. This article first appeared in *Christian Century* (January 4, 1967).

3. Ibid., 38.

4. Josiah Young describes this period as a sacred time because it was the cauldron out of which African American culture was shaped. See his *Black and African Theologies: Siblings or Distant Cousins?* (Maryknoll: Orbis Books, 1986).

5. Winthrop Jordan, *White Over Black: American Attitudes Toward the Negro, 1550–1812* (Chapel Hill: University of North Carolina Press, 1968), 220–21.

6. Thomas Jefferson, "Notes on the State of Virginia" (written in 1782, first published in 1787); excerpt in *A Documentary History of Slavery in North America*, Willie Lee Rose, ed. (New York: Oxford University Press, 1976), 202.

7. James Oakes, *The Ruling Race: A History of American Slaveholders* (New York: Vintage Books, 1982), 3.

8. John W. Blassingame, *The Slave Community: Plantation Life in the Antebellum South*, rev. and enlarged edition (New York: Oxford University Press, 1979), 80.

9. Samuel D. How, *Slaveholding Not Sinful: Slavery The Punishment of Man's Sin, Its Remedy, The Gospel of Christ* (New Brunswick, N.J.: Terhunes Press, 1856; repr., Freeport, New York: Books for Libraries Press, 1971).

10. H. Shelton Smith, *In His Image But: Racism in Southern Religion, 1780–1910* (Durham: Duke University Press, 1972), 153.

11. Albert J. Raboteau, *Slave Religion: The "Invisible Institution" in*

the Antebellum South (New York: Oxford University Press, 1978), 98f.

12. See, for example, Romans 2:11; 10:12; Galatians 3:28; Colossians 3:11.

13. Raboteau, *Slave Religion*, 102.

14. Smith, *In His Image But*, 135.

15. How, *Slaveholding*, 24.

16. Smith, *In His Image But*, 134.

17. *Slave Testimony*, John W. Blassingame, ed. (Baton Rouge: Louisiana State University Press, 1977), 420.

18. Quoted in H. Richard Niebuhr, *The Social Sources of Denominationalism* (Cleveland: Meridian Books, 1929), 249.

19. "The Carolina Chronicle of Dr. Francis Le Jau, 1706–1717," Frank W. Klingberg, ed. (Berkeley: University of California Press, 1956) in *Afro-American Religious History*, Milton Sernett, ed. (Durham: Duke University Press, 1985), 25.

20. Blassingame, *Slave Testimony*, 420.

21. Ibid., 411.

22. Frederick Douglass, "Slaveholding Religion and the Christianity of Christ," in Sernett, *Afro-American Religious History*, 101.

23. Ibid.

24. Raboteau, *Slave Religion*, 177.

25. Ibid., 213–14.

26. Ibid., 212.

27. Cecil Cone, *The Identity Crisis in Black Theology* (Nashville: AMEC, 1975), 37.

28. John Lovell, Jr., *Black Song: The Forge and the Flame* (New York: Macmillan, 1972), 303.

29. Thurman, *Deep River and the Negro Spiritual Speaks of Life and Death* (Richmond, Indiana: Friends United Press, 1975), 26.

30. James Cone, *The Spirituals and the Blues* (New York: The Seabury Press, 1972; Maryknoll, N.Y.: Orbis Books, 1991), 54.

31. For more information on the carryovers from African religion, see Sterling Stuckey, *Slave Culture: Nationalist Theory and the Foundations of Black America* (New York: Oxford University Press, 1987).

32. Cone, *Spirituals and Blues*, 51.

33. Raboteau, *Slave Religion*, 260.

34. Lovell, *Black Song*, 235.

35. It should be noted that this belief is also compatible with the African religious belief that the ancestors are still very much a part of the present. For more on this, see Stuckey, *Slave Culture*.

36. Lovell, *Black Song*, 232.

37. Ibid.

38. Thurman, *Deep River*, 33.

39. For a discussion of the ambiguous nature of the meaning of freedom in the spirituals, see Raboteau, *Slave Religion*, 248ff.

40. See, for example, Thomas Wentworth Higginson, "Slave Songs and Spirituals," "Negro Spirituals," *Atlantic Monthly* 19:16 (June 1867) in *Afro-American Religious History*, Sernett, ed., 128ff.

41. Howard Thurman, *Jesus and the Disinherited* (Richmond, Indiana: Friends United Press, 1949), 31.

42. Levine, *Black Culture and Black Consciousness*, 51.

43. Lovell, *Black Song*, 235.

44. Raboteau, *Slave Religion*, 318.

45. Quoted in Levine, *Black Culture and Black Consciousness*, 50; see also Eugene Genovese, *Roll Jordan Roll: The World the Slaves Made* (New York: Vintage Books, 1974), 252–55.

46. Raboteau, *Slave Religion*, 318,

47. Blassingame, *Slave Testimony*, 56.

48. Douglass, "Slaveholding Religion," in Sernett, *Afro-American Religious History*, 104–6.

49. Blassingame, *Slave Testimony*, 51.

50. For a good discussion of Black nationalism in America, see *Black Nationalism in America*, John H. Bracey, Jr., August Meier, and Elliot Rudwick, eds. (Indianapolis: Bobbs Merrill Educational Publishing, 1970); Alphonso Pinkey, *Red, Black and Green: Black Nationalism in the United States* (Cambridge: Cambridge University Press, 1976).

51. Robert Alexander Young, "The Ethiopian Manifesto" (New York: 1829), repr. in *The Ideological Origins of Black Nationalism*, Sterling Stuckey, ed. (Boston: Beacon Press, 1972), 33–34.

52. Ibid., 37.

53. *Respect Black: The Writings and Speeches of Henry McNeal Turner*, Edwin Redkey, ed. (New York: Arno Press, 1971), 176.

54. *Philosophy and Opinions of Marcus Garvey*, Amy Jacques-Garvey, ed. (New York: Atheneum, 1986), 1:44.

55. Randall K. Burkett, *Garveyism as a Religious Movement* (Metuchen, N.J.: Scarecrow Press, 1978), 53.

56. Ibid., 53.

57. Langston Hughes, *The Panther and the Lash: Poems of Our Times* (New York: Alfred A. Knopf, 1969), 37.

58. Countee Cullen, *The Black Christ* (New York: Harper and Brothers, 1928), 77.

59. Countee Cullen, "Heritage," in *Color* (New York: Harper and Brothers, 1925), 36–41.

60. John Henrik Clarke, "The Boy Who Painted Christ Black," in

Black Culture: Reading and Writing Black, Gloria M. Simmons and Helene D. Hutchinson, eds. (New York: Holt Rinehart and Winston, 1972), 163ff.

CHAPTER 2

1. *New Black Voices: An Anthology of Contemporary Afro-American Literature*, Abraham Chapman, ed. (New York: Mentor, 1972), 44.

2. Imamu Amiri Baraka, "Sacred Chant for the Return of Black Spirit and Power," in *New Black Voices*, Chapman, 209.

3. King, "Playboy Interview," repr. in *A Testament of Hope: The Essential Writings of Martin Luther King, Jr.*, James M. Washington, ed. (New York: Harper and Row, 1986), 345.

4. See, for instance, "I Have a Dream" (Washington, August 28, 1963), "Our God Is Marching!" (Selma, Alabama, March 25, 1965), and "Nobel Prize Acceptance" (Oslo, Norway, December 10, 1964) reprinted in *A Testament of Hope*, Washington, ed.

5. The precise designation "kitchen table experience" is taken from David Garrow, *Bearing the Cross: Martin Luther King, Jr., and the Southern Christian Leadership Conference* (New York: William Morrow, 1986).

6. Martin Luther King, Jr., *Stride Toward Freedom: The Montgomery Story* (New York: Harper and Row, 1958), 3.

7. Ibid., 135.

8. James Cone, "The Theology of Martin King, Jr.," *Union Theological Seminary Quarterly Review* 40, no. 4 (1986), 127.

9. Garrow, *Bearing the Cross*, 58.

10. King, "Eulogy for the Martyred Children" (September 15, 1963), repr. in *Testament of Hope*, Washington, 222.

11. King, "Remaining Awake Through a Great Revolution" (Washington Cathedral, Washington, D.C., March 31, 1968), repr. in *Testament of Hope*, Washington, 268–78.

12. King, "The Death of Evil Upon the Seashore," in *Strength to Love* (Philadelphia: Fortress Press, 1963), 83. Emphasis added.

13. Ibid., 76–85.

14. Ibid., 84. Emphasis added.

15. King, "Facing the Challenge of a New Age" (First Annual Institute on Non-Violence for Social Change, December, 1956), repr. in *Testament of Hope*, Washington, 133–44.

16. King, "I Have A Dream," ibid., 220.

17. Wyatt Tee Walker, *Somebody's Calling My Name: Black Sacred Music and Social Change* (Valley Forge, Pa.: Judson Press, 1979), 154f.

18. King, "Playboy Interview," *Playboy* (January 1965), repr. in *Testament of Hope*, Washington, 348.

19. See, for instance, King, "The Power of Nonviolence" (YMCA and YWCA at the University of California, Berkeley, June 4, 1957); "The American Dream" (Commencement Address at Lincoln University in Pennsylvania, June 6, 1961), ibid.

20. Amos 5:24.

21. King, "Address to the Initial Mass Meeting of the Montgomery Improvement Association" (Holt Street Baptist Church, December 5, 1955, King Center Archives).

22. Ibid.

23. King, *Stride Toward Freedom*, 93. It should also be noted that when King entered the protest movement and began to clarify the inseparable link between Christianity and protest against injustice, the Black church was thought by some to be in a state of "deradicalization." Gayraud Wilmore said that at the end of World War I "independent Black churches were becoming respectable institutions . . . they moved more amd more toward what was presented by the White churches as the model of authentic Christian faith." This deradicalization continued, Wilmore says, until King entered the civil rights movement and "reversed the trend and gave new vitality and relevance to black Christianity in the United States." See Wilmore, *Black Religion and Black Radicalism: An Interpretation of the Religious History of Afro-American People*, 2nd rev. edit. (Maryknoll, N.Y.: Orbis Books, 1983), 142ff.; 174ff. James Cone made a similar point. He said, "King put the connection between religion and politics back into the Black Church" (personal interview, July 2, 1985). J. Metz Rollins, the first chairperson of the National Committee of Black Churchmen, credited King for bringing a "dignity" back to the Black church (personal interview, January 9, 1986).

24. King, "Remaining Awake Through a Storm" (Washington, March 31, 1968), repr. in *Testament of Hope*, Washington, 275.

25. Alex Haley, *The Autobiography of Malcolm X* (New York: Ballantine Books, 1965), 200–201.

26. See the series, "God's Angry Men," *New York Amsterdam News*, April 27, 1957; 18.

27. See the series, "God's Angry Men", *New York Amsterdam News*, May 18, 1957; 5.

28. Ibid.

29. This question is paraphrased from a question Mary Daly raises concerning the patriarchal nature of Christianity. See her *Beyond God the Father: Toward a Philosophy of Women's Liberation* (Boston: Beacon Press, 1973), 72ff.

30. For more concerning Kenneth Clark's views on the impact of White racism on Black development, see Kenneth B. Clark, *Dark Ghetto: Dilemmas of Social Power* (New York: Harper Torchbooks, 1965).

31. Hegeman in Louis Lomax and Mike Wallace, "The Hate that Hate Produced" Television Series, July, 1959.

32. See Julius Lester, "The Angry Children of Malcolm X" in *Black Protest Thought in the Twentieth Century*, 2nd edition, August Meier, Elliot Rudwick, and Francis Broderick, eds. (Indianapolis: Bobbs-Merrill Educational Publishing, 1971), 469-84.

33. See "Nonviolence is the Foundation," ibid., 307.

34. See David Garrow's discussion of King's acceptance of nonviolence as a strategy and eventual way of life in *Bearing the Cross*, 68, 72ff.

35. This was King's designation for the kingdom of God.

36. King, *Stride for Freedom*, 220.

37. Vincent Harding, "The Religion of Black Power," in *The Religious Situation: 1968*, Donald R. Cutler, ed. (Boston: Beacon Press, 1968), 4.

38. Lester, "The Angry Children of Malcolm X" in *Black Protest Thought*, Meier, Rudwick, and Broderick, eds. 482.

39. Metz Rollins (personal interview, January 6, 1986).

40. "Statement by the National Committee of Negro Churchmen," *New York Times* (July 31, 1966), repr. in *Black Theology: Documentary History*, Wilmore and Cone, eds., 24.

41. Ibid.

42. "Statement by the National Committee of Black Churchmen," June 13, 1969, repr. in *Black Theology: Documentary History*, Wilmore and Cone, eds., 101.

CHAPTER 3

1. Joseph Johnson, Jr., "Jesus the Liberator," in J. Deotis Roberts and J. Gardiner, eds., *Quest for a Black Theology* (Philadelphia: Pilgrim Press, 1971), 101.

2. Cleage quoted in Alex Poinsett, "The Quest for a Black Messiah," *Ebony* (March 1969), 176.

3. Albert Cleage, *The Black Messiah* (Kansas City: Sheed and Ward, 1969), 42.

4. Ibid., 3.

5. Ibid., 42.

6. Ibid., pp. 42-43.

7. "The Black Messiah and the Black Revolution," in *Quest for a Black Theology*, Roberts and Gardiner, eds., 11.

8. Cleage, *The Black Messiah*, 3.

9. See Cleage's *Black Christian Nationalism: New Directions for the Black Church* (New York: William Morrow, 1972); "A Black Man's View of Authority" in *Erosion of Authority*, C. Manschreck, ed. (Nashville: Abingdon Press, 1971), 59–71.

10. See Hiley H. Ward, *Prophet of the Black Nation*, (Philadelphia: Pilgrim Press, 1969), esp. chap. 1.

11. Paul Tillich, *Dynamics of Faith* (New York: Harper Colophon Books, 1957), 42–43; for an analysis of Cone's use of Tillich, see Robinson B. James, "A Tillichian Analysis of James Cone's Black Theology," *Perspective in Religious Studies* 1 (Spring 1974), 15–28.

12. Cone, *Black Theology of Liberation* (Philadelphia: Lippincott Press, 1970); second edition (Maryknoll, New York: Orbis Books, 1986), 213.

13. Cone, *God of the Oppressed* (New York: Seabury Press, 1975), 136.

14. See, for example, J. Deotis Roberts, "A Critique of James Cone's *God of the Oppressed*," in *Journal of the Interdenominational Theological Center* 3 (Fall 1975), 58–63. Each time that I have taught Black theology to seminary students, some of them have consistently critiqued what they believed to be Cone's literal and exclusive identification of Christ as Black.

15. Cone and William Hordern, "Dialogue on Black Theology," in *The Christian Century* (September 15, 1971), 1084.

16. See Cone's discussion of his disillusionment with Christian theology in *My Soul Looks Back* (Nashville: Abingdon, 1982), esp. chap. 2.

17. Cone, *Black Theology of Liberation*, second edition, 144, note 5.

18. Roberts, *Black Political Theology* (Philadelphia: Westminster Press, 1974), 134.

19. Roberts, "Black Theology and the Theological Revolution," *Journal of Religious Thought* 28 (Spring-Summer 1972), 16.

20. Roberts, *Liberation and Reconciliation: A Black Theology* (Philadelphia: Westminster Press, 1971), 137.

21. See Cecil Cone, *The Identity Crisis in Black Theology* (Nashville: African Methodist Episcopal Church, 1975); James Cone, "An Interpretation of the Debate among Black Theologians," in Wilmore and Cone, eds., *Black Theology: A Documentary History*, 609–23.

22. Roberts, telephone interview, March 11, 1988.

23. Roberts, *Black Political Theology*, 119.

24. See page 35 above.

25. Roberts, telephone interview, March 11, 1988.

26. A good discussion of the NCBC influence on Black theology is found in Gayraud Wilmore, *Black Religion and Black Radicalism*, second revised edition (Maryknoll, New York: Orbis Books, 1983). See also James Cone, *For My People* (Maryknoll, New York: Orbis Books, 1984), chap. 1.

27. Roberts, "Black Consciousness in Theological Perspective," in *Quest for a Black Theology*, 63.

28. *The Black Messiah*, 73.

29. Ibid., 3.

30. Ibid., 73.

31. Ibid., 93.

32. Ibid., 186.

33. Ibid., 198.

34. Ibid.

35. Exodus 19:4–5, quoted by Cone in *God of the Oppressed*, 64.

36. Ibid.

37. Ibid., 119.

38. Ibid., 135.

39. Ibid.

40. "Black Theology and Black Liberation," *The Christian Century* 87 (September 16, 1970), 1087.

41. *Black Theology and Black Power* (New York: Seabury Press, 1969), 1.

42. *Liberation and Reconciliation*, 59.

43. Ibid., 29.

44. *Black Political Theology*, 133.

45. Ibid., 153.

46. Ibid., 152.

47. Ibid., 182.

48. *The Black Messiah*, 214.

49. See especially *God of the Oppressed*. See also "A Critique of J. Deotis Roberts, Sr. A Black Political Theology," *Journal of the Interdenominational Theological Center* 3 (Fall 1975), 55–57; "Theological Reflections on Reconciliation," *Christianity and Crisis* 32 (January 22, 1973), 303–8.

50. 2 Corinthians 5:19 quoted by Cone, *God of the Oppressed*, 228.

51. Ibid., 236.

52. See, for instance, William Robert Miller, *Nonviolence: A Christian Interpretation* (New York: Schocken Books, 1964).

53. *The Black Messiah*, 202.

54. Ibid., 98.

55. *God of the Oppressed*, 222.

56. *Liberation and Reconciliation*, 191–92.

57. Roberts, "Black Theology and the Theological Revolution," 17.

CHAPTER 4

1. Cone, *For My People*, 36.

2. Cleage, *Black Christian Nationalism*, xv.

3. Roberts, "Black Theology and the Theological Revolution," 171.

4. See, for instance, Gayraud Wilmore, "The Black Messiah: Revising the Color Symbolism of Western Christology," *Journal of the Interdenominational Center* 2 (Fall 1975), 13.

5. See, for instance, Cain Felder, *Troubling Biblical Waters: Race, Class, and Family* (Maryknoll, N.Y.: Orbis Books, 1989); see also Martin Bernal, *Black Athena: The Afroasiatic Roots of Classical Civilization*, vol. 1, *The Fabrication of Ancient Greece 1785–1985* (London: Free Association Books, 1987).

6. See, for instance, the Anchor Bible commentaries, Joseph A. Fitzmeyer, *The Gospel According to Luke* (Garden City, New York: Doubleday, 1981), esp. 497–98; see also Hans Conzelman, *Jesus*, trans. by J. Raymond Lord (Philadelphia: Fortress Press, 1973).

7. See Wilmore's discussion of the "whitenizing" of Christian symbols in "The Black Messiah: Revising the Color Symbolism of Western Christology," in *Journal of the Interdenominational Theological Center* 2 (Fall 1974), 8-18.

8. "Pastoral Ministry in the Origin and Development of Black Theology," in *The Journal of the Interdenominational Theological Center* (Spring 1986), 216.

9. Ibid., 222.

10. See West, "The Crisis in Theological Education," in *Prophetic Fragments*, 273–80.

11. See Wiley, "Black Theology, Black Church, and the African American Community," in James Cone and Gayraud Wilmore, eds., *Black Theology: A Documentary History* volume two: 1980–1992 (Maryknoll, N.Y.: Orbis Books, 1993), 127–38.

12. Joyce Ladner, previously a member of SNCC and now vice-president of Academic Affairs at Howard University, recalled that she did not have any negative reactions to the fact that she and other SNCC women were not asked to speak at the march. She said that they were more concerned that John Lewis be able to speak, since they viewed him as their leader (telephone interview, January 11, 1986). Gloria

Richardson recalled that "all those male leaders" of the march were initially going to allow her ten minutes to speak, but they became afraid of what she might say. She said that when she finally got to the dais there was not a chair for her (personal interview, January 9, 1986).

13. Hedgeman, *The Gift of Chaos* (New York: Oxford University Press, 1977), 86; see also Hedgeman's account in *The Trumpet Sounds: A Memoir of Negro Leadership* (New York: Holt Rinehart and Winston, 1964), 178ff.

14. Cited in Helen King, "Black Woman?," *Ebony* (March 1971), 68.

15. Ibid., 70.

16. Ibid., 71; for further reactions to White feminism, see also Toni Morrison, "What the Black Woman Thinks about Women's Lib," in *New York Times Magazine* (August 22, 1971).

17. I have said more about the significance of Black women's stance in relationship to their own oppression vis-à-vis their commitment to the Black freedom struggle in other places. See, for instance, "Womanist Theology: What Is Its Relationship to Black Theology?" in James Cone and Gayraud Wilmore, *Black Theology : A Documentary History* vol. two (Maryknoll, N.Y.: Orbis Books, 1993), 290–99.

18. This is evidenced in their consistent use of gender exclusive language, but most prominently in the Black theological statements that emerged from NCBC. The June 13, 1989 Black Theology statement by the National Committee of Black Churchmen clearly defined Black liberation in terms of achieving manhood. See Cone and Wilmore, *Black Theology: A Documentary History*, vol. one, 1966–1979 (Maryknoll, N.Y.: Orbis Books, 1993), 37–39.

19. While the term *womanist* has only recently emerged, certainly the Black woman's consciousness, which emerged out of the civil rights/Black Power movement, is the precursor of womanist thought. The term *womanist* originated with Alice Walker's interpretation of the Black cultural expression, "You acting womanish." Womanish, according to Walker, refers to audacious, courageous, or willful behavior. Drawing upon womanish, Walker provides a four-part definition of a womanist. A womanist, she explains, "loves other women, sexually and/or non-sexually," is "committed to survival and wholeness of entire people, male and females," is "not a separatist, except periodically, for health." She loves the moon, the folk, roundness, the spirit, and she "loves herself, regardless." Walker concludes the definition by saying "Womanist is to feminist as purple to lavender." See Walker, *In Search of Our Mothers' Gardens* (New York: Harcourt Brace Jovanovich, 1983). Although the meaning of the term *womanist* originated with Walker's

definition for Black women, particularly Black female religious scholars, it now goes beyond her words. It points to the richness and complexity of being Black and female in a society that tends to devalue both Blackness and womanhood. Womanist sybolizes Black women's experience of struggle against their multidimensional oppression. In religious and theological scholarship, womanist signals understandings of the Bible, church, God, and Jesus Christ, which have emerged from the social-historical contexts of Black women struggling to survive with dignity and to be free.

20. See C. Eric Lincoln and Lawrence H. Mamiya, *The Black Church in the African American Experience* (Durham, N.C.: Duke University Press, 1990), 274ff.

21. Jacquelyn Grant, "Black Theology and the Black Woman" in Cone and Wilmore, eds., *Black Theology: A Documentary History*, 418–43.

22. bell hooks, *Ain't I a Woman?*, 124.

23. For a more extended analysis of the women's movements in relation to Black women, see Angela Davis, *Women, Race, and Class* (New York: Random House, 1981); Paula Giddings, *When and Where I Enter: The Impact of Black Women on Race and Sex in America* (New York: William Morrow, 1984).

24. Mary Daly, *gyn/Ecology: The Metaethics of Radical Feminism* (Boston, Beacon Press, 1978).

25. Audre Lorde, "An Open Letter to Mary Daly," in Cherrie Moraga and Gloria Anzulda, eds., *This Bridge Called my Back* (New York: Kitchen Table Press, 1983), 95.

26. Ibid., 96.

27. Delores Williams, "Women's Oppression and Life-Line Politics in Black Women's Religious Narratives," *Journal of Feminist Studies in Religion* (Fall 1985), 59–71.

28. "Feminist Theology in The Academy," *Christianity and Crisis* vol. 45 no. 3 (March 4, 1985), 57–62.

29. Delores Williams, "The Color of Feminism," *Christianity and Crisis* 45, no. 7 (April 29, 1985), 165.

30. See *Sexism and God-Talk: Toward a Feminist Theology* (Boston: Beacon Press, 1983), esp. chap. 5, "Christology: Can a Male Jesus Save Women?"

31. See Daly, *Beyond God the Father: Toward a Philosophy of Women's Liberation* (Boston: Beacon Press, 1973), esp. chap. 3, "Beyond Christology: A World without Model."

32. See Jacquelyn Grant, *White Women's Christ and Black Women's Jesus: Feminist Christology and Womanist Response* (Atlanta: Scholars Press, 1989).

CHAPTER 5

1. Walker, *In Search of Our Mothers' Gardens* (New York: Harcourt Brace Jovanovich, Publishers, 1983), xi.

2. Ibid., xi.

3. Ibid.

4. Sanders, "Christian Ethics and Theology in Womanist Perspective," in *Journal of Feminist Studies in Religion*, vol. 5, no. 2 (Fall 1989), 90.

5. See Patricia Hill Collins, *Black Feminist Thought: Knowledge, Consciousness, and the Politics of Empowerment* (New York: Routledge, 1991), 194.

6. Ibid.

7. Ibid.

8. This general assembly was held in Oaxtepec, Mexico, December 7–14, 1986. I have discussed the women's dialogue in Oaxtepec in "Reflections on the Second General Assembly of EATWOT" in *Third World Theologies: Commonalities and Divergences*, K. C. Abraham, ed. (Maryknoll, New York: Orbis Books, 1990), 174–79.

9. Sojourner Truth, "Ain't I a Woman" (1851), in Miriam Schneir, ed., *Feminism: The Essential Historical Writings* (New York: Vintage Books, 1972), 95.

10. In previous writings I have labeled this a "spirituality of survival." Informed by what Patricia Hill Collins describes as a "culture of resistance," which Black women have nurtured, I now describe this as a "spirituality of resistance." The term "resistance" implies more than just finding a way to exist, but it also suggests fighting back against that which is oppressive. Resistance suggests a more active image than perhaps suggested by the term *survival.*

11. *Maria W. Stewart, America's First Black Woman Political Writer: Essays and Speeches*, Marilyn Richardson, ed. (Bloomington: Indiana University Press, 1987), 50.

12. Ibid., 29.

13. See page 27 and 43 above where I mentioned that the slaves saw Jesus in the line of Moses, and King understood him in the line of Amos.

14. See, for instance, Paul Tillich's discussion of religious symbols in *Dynamics of Faith* (New York: Harper Colophon Books, Harper and Row Publishers, 1957). See esp. Chapter III "Symbols of Faith," 41–54.

15. See, for instance, *White Women's Christ and Black Women's Jesus:*

Feminist Christology and Womanist Response (Atlanta: Scholars Press, 1989); "Womanist Theology: Black Women's Experience as a Source for Doing Theology, with Special Reference to Christology," *Journal of the Interdenominational Theological Center* vol. 13, no. 2 (Spring 1986), 195–212.

16. "Womanist Theology . . . with Special Reference to Christology," 210.

17. Williams, "Black Women's Surrogacy Experience and the Christian Notion of Redemption," in *After Patriarchy: Feminist Transformations of the World Religions*, Paula M. Cooey, William R. Eakin, and Jay B. McDaniel, eds. (Maryknoll, N.Y.: Orbis Books, 1991), 9.

18. Richard A. Norris, trans. and ed., *The Christological Controversy* (Philadelphia: Fortress Press, 1980), 3.

19. Ibid., 2.

20. Patricia Hill Collins, *Black Feminist Thought: Knowledge, Consciousness and the Politics of Empowerment* (New York: Routledge, Chapman and Hall, Inc.) 31–32.

21. I have discussed an appropriate methodology for teaching womanist theology in the seminary in "Teaching Womanist Theology: A Case Study" in *Journal of Feminist Studies in Religion* vol. 8 no. 2 (Fall 1992).

22. Alice Walker, *The Color Purple* (New York: Washington Square Press, Pocket Books, 1982), 177.

Index

Afrocentrism, 104, 118n2
AIDS, 4, 99
American Academy of Religion, 114
Amos, 43, 107
Ashe, Arthur, 5
Baker, Ella, 88
Baptism, 17
Baraka, Imamu Amiri, 36
Bates, Daisy, 90
Bibb, Henry, 28, 29
Black Christ, 5-8, 20, 24, 27-37, 44-45, 48-50, 52, 54-55, 72-73, 77, 84-88, 90, 97; Cleage's version of, 55-58, 66, 73-74, 79-80; Cone's version of, 58-60, 66, 69, 75-76, 82-84; Roberts's version of, 60-64, 72, 76-77, 80-82; womanist perspective on, 104, 106-110, 116-117
Black Christianity, 3
Black church, 3, 4, 56, 86-88, 93, 114-116
Black clergy, 51-52
Black liberation, 66, 72-73, 75-76, 82, 86-88
Black literature, 32-34, 36
Black Messiah, 57, 61, 80
Black nationalism, 30-32, 36, 45, 56-58, 84
Black oppression, 98-99, 107
Black Power movement, 6, 34, 35, 48, 50-52, 63, 69, 75, 85, 88, 89
Black theologians, 7, 54, 84, 91-92
Black theology, 6-7, 10, 34, 78-79, 87
Black Theology of Liberation, A (Cone), 3
Black women, 4, 30, 88-96, 97-99, 102-116
Black Woman (Cade), 92
Blackness, 34-35, 60, 64, 78, 81, 84-85
Blackwell, Unita, 89
Brooks, Gwendolyn, 90
Bogg, Susan, 17
Cade, Toni, 92
Carmichael, Stokely, 35, 57
Christ, 3; Blackness of, 4, 7-8, 29, 33-34, 37, 55-64, 78; Black understanding of, 3-4; as Black woman, 109; as Liberator, 52, 67-69, 107; universality of, 62, 80. See also Black Christ; Jesus; White Christ
Christology, 110-113
Civil Rights movement, 35, 37-45, 85, 88, 89
Clark, Kenneth, 47
Clarke, John Henrik, 33
Cleage, Albert, 7, 54, 60, 62-64, 67-72, 77-78, 91; assessment of, 79-80; on Blackness of

Christ, 55-58; on liberation and reconciliation, 64-66; on violence, 73-74
Collins, Patricia Hill, 101, 113, 130n10
Color (Cullen), 33
Color Purple, The (Walker), 117
Cone, James, 3, 7, 22, 54, 55, 61-63, 73, 78, 91; on Blackness of Christ, 58-60; critical assessment of, 82-84; on liberation and reconciliation, 66-69; on violence, 75-77
Cross, 22-23, 49, 68, 71
Crucifixion, 21-22, 24, 68, 71, 81
Cullen, Countee, 33
Daly, Mary, 94-95
Daniel, 27
Douglass, Frederick, 18, 19, 28
Ebony magazine, 9
Ecumenical Association of Third World Theologians (EATWOT), 102-103
Eichleberger, William, 7
Ethiopian Manifesto (Young), 31
Exodus, 26-27, 40-41, 64, 67, 69-70
Felder, Cain Hope, 1
Feminist theology, 93-96, 103
For Colored Girls Who Have Considered Suicide When the Rainbow IS Enuf (Shange), 92
Freedom, 24-25, 30, 38, 41-43, 46
Garrow, David, 40
Garvey, Marcus, 32, 58
Gays, discrimination against, 4, 99-101, 105. *See also* lesbians
Giovanni, Nikki, 90
God, as Black, 32, 64, 66; acts in history, 26-27, 29, 38-41, 43, 64-65, 67, 70; in relation with Black people, 39
Grant, Jacquelyn, 93, 95, 109

gyn/Ecology (Daly), 94
Ham, 15
Hamer, Fannie Lou, 89, 108
Harding, Vincent, 9
Hedgeman, Anna Arnold, 47, 89
Henry, Milton, 57
Henry, Richard, 57
Heterosexism, 99, 101
Homophobia, 100
hooks, bell, 94
Hoover, Theressa, 92
Hughes, Langston, 32
Incarnation, 61
Jefferson, Thomas, 11
Jenkins, Emma, 89
Jesus, 10, 13, 14, 20; Blackness of, 47, 56-58, 79; as incarnation of God, 37; liberating ministry of, 15-17, 19, 21, 23-24, 27-29, 31, 34, 37, 43-44, 65, 75, 81-82, 91-92; and slaves, 20-27
Jonah, 27
Johnson, Joseph, Jr., 53
Jones, Leroi. *See* Baraka, Imamu Amiri
Jones, Major, 7
King, Martin Luther, Jr., 6, 36, 37, 48-52, 71-73, 88, 107, 123n23; and the Black Christ, 37-45; on freedom, 41-43; on God, 38-41
Kings, Annie Mae, 89
Ladner, Joyce, 127n12
Lee, Jareena, 109
Lesbians, discrimination against, 4, 99-102, 105. *See also* gays
Lewis, John, 127n12
Linnaeus, Carolus, 11
Lomax, Louis, 47
Lorde, Audre, 94-95
Lovell, John, 24
Marxism, 98
Mary, 55

Moses, 27, 43, 107
Nash, Diane, 89
National Conference of Black
    Churchmen (NCBC), 51-52,
    63
Nicene/Chalcedonian tradition,
    111-113
Nonviolence, 48-50, 73-76
Parks, Rosa, 89-90
Paul, 25, 16, 25-26
Prosser, Gabriel, 3, 25
Racism. *See* White racism
Raboteau, Albert, 14, 27
Randolph, A. Philip, 89
Reconciliation, 69-72, 76-77, 82
Religio-Cultural Analysis, 104-
    106
Resurrection, 65-66, 68-69, 81
Richardson, Gloria, 88, 127n12
Roberts, J. Deotis, 7, 54, 55, 73,
    78, 79, 90; on Blackness of
    Christ, 60-63; critical
    assessment of, 80-82; on
    liberation and reconciliation,
    69-72; on violence, 76-77
Robinson, Joann, 89
Ruether, Rosemary, 95
Rush, Benjamin, 11
Saunders, Cheryl, 100-101
Sexuality, 99-102
Shange, Ntozake, 92
Simon the Cyrenian, 32
Slavery, 10, 12-30; cruelty of, 17-
    20; justification of, 12-14
Slave Christianity, 10, 20-30, 38,
    43, 45, 47, 59, 107
Slave songs (spirituals), 21-26,
    42
Slaveholding Christianity, 10, 12-
    14, 25, 46, 57, 65, 83
Smith, H. Shelton, 15
Smith, Ruby Doris, 89
Southern Christian Leadership

Conference (SCLC), 88
Spirituality of resistance, 105-106
Stewart, Maria, 105-106
Social-political analysis, 97-99,
    102-104
Student Non-Violent
    Coordinating Committee
    (SNCC), 48, 50, 88, 89, 127n12
Thurman, Howard, 22, 26
Tillich, Paul, 58
Third World women, 102-103
Truth, Sojourner, 25, 103, 108,
    109
Tubman, Harriet, 25, 98, 108
Turner, Henry McNeal, 31
Turner, Nat, 3, 25
Van Dyke, Charlie, 20
Vesey, Denmark, 3, 25
Violence, 73-76, 81-82
Walker, Alice, 98, 100, 117,
    129n19
Wallace, Mike, 47
West, Cornel, 3, 87
White Christ, 4-5, 9-10, 12-20,
    36-38, 47, 50, 53, 57, 63, 81,
    83, 84, 86, 115
White Racism, 2-6, 36, 38-39,
    41, 48, 50, 53, 57, 59, 69, 72-
    74, 76, 85, 89, 93, 107, 116
Wholeness, 98, 102-104
Wiley, Dennis, 87
Williams, Delores, 95, 110
Wilmore, Gayraud, 7, 87
Womanist, definition of, 128n19
Womanist theology, 8, 92-96,
    100-102, 103, 106-111, 113-
    117
Women. *See* Black women
X, Malcolm, 1, 6, 9, 19, 36, 37,
    45, 50, 52, 54, 57, 64, 66, 69,
    73, 84, 115, 116; and
    Christianity, 46-48
Young, Robert Alexander, 31